# DEVELOPING LITERACY

**100% NEW**

**Photocopiable teaching resources for literacy**

# CREATING AND SHAPING TEXTS

**Ages 9–10**

**Christine Moorcroft**

D1102749

A & C Black • London

**Please check front pocket for CD**

# Contents

## Narrative

### Novels and stories by significant children's authors

### Traditional stories, fables, myths, legends

### Stories from other cultures

### Older literature

# Poetry

## Poetic style

## Classic/narrative poems

## Choral and performance

---

Published 2008 by A & C Black Publishers Limited
36 Soho Square, London W1D 3QY
www.acblack.com

ISBN 978-1-4081-0032-5

Copyright text © Christine Moorcroft 2008
Copyright illustrations © Adrian Barclay 2008
Copyright cover illustration © Piers Baker 2008
Editor: Jane Klima
Designed by Bob Vickers

The author and publishers would like to thank Ray Barker and Rifat Siddiqui for their advice in producing this series of books.

A CIP catalogue record for this book is available from the British Library.

The author and publishers are grateful for permission to reproduce the following: p15, extract from *The Water Horse* by Dick King-Smith (Puffin), used by permission of A P Watt Ltd; p16, extract from *The Sheep-Pig* by Dick King-Smith (Puffin), used by permission of A P Watt Ltd; p17, extract from *Just William on Holiday* by Richmal Crompton (Macmillan), used by permission of A P Watt Ltd on behalf of Dr Paul Asbee; pp25-26, extract from *Parvana's Journey* by Deborah Ellis (OUP), used by permission of Oxford University Press; p31, extract from *Just William at Christmas* by Richmal Crompton (Macmillan), used by permission of A P Watt Ltd on behalf of Dr Paul Ashbee; p55,'Early Country Village Morning' by Grace Nichols, © Grace Nichols 1988, reproduced by permission of Curtis Brown Group Ltd, London; p56, 'Taking my Pen for a Walk' by Julie O'Callaghan, used by permission of the author; p57, 'The Listeners' by Walter de la Mare, used by permission of the Literary Trustees of Walter de la Mare and the Society of Authors as their representative. Every effort has been made to trace copyright holders and to obtain their permission for use of copyright material. The author and publishers would be pleased to rectify any error or omission in future editions.

Printed and bound in Great Britain by Halstan Printing Group, Amersham, Buckinghamshire.

A & C Black uses paper produced with elemental chlorine-free pulp, harvested from managed sustainable forests.

# Introduction

*100% New Developing Literacy Creating and Shaping Texts* is a series of seven photocopiable activity books for developing children's understanding of the structures and purposes of different types of text and their skills in organising and writing texts.

The books provide learning activities to support strands 9 and 10 (Creating and shaping texts and Text structure and organisation) of the literacy objectives of the Primary Framework for Literacy and Mathematics.

The structure of *100% New Developing Literacy Creating and Shaping Texts: Ages 9–10* complements the structure of the Primary Framework and includes the range of text types suggested in the planning for activities for children aged 9–10. It focuses on the following types of text:

- Narrative (Novels and stories by significant children's authors; Traditional stories, fables, myths, legends; Stories from other cultures; Older literature; Film narrative)
- Non-fiction (Instructions; Recounts; Persuasive writing)
- Poetry (Poetic style; Classic/narrative poems; Choral and performance).

*100% New Developing Literacy Creating and Shaping Texts: Ages 9–10* addresses the following learning objectives from the Primary Framework for Literacy:

Strand 9 Creating and shaping texts

- Reflect independently and critically on their own writing and edit and improve it
- Experiment with different narrative forms and styles to write their own stories
- Adapt non-narrative forms and styles to write fiction or factual texts, including poems
- Vary the pace and develop the viewpoint through the use of direct and reported speech, portrayal of action and selection of detail
- Create multi-layered texts, including use of hyperlinks and linked web pages.

Strand 10 Text structure and organisation

- Experiment with the order of sections and paragraphs to achieve different effects
- Change the order of material within a paragraph, moving the topic sentence.

## The activities

Some activities can be carried out with the whole class, some are more suitable for small groups and others are for individual work. It is important that the children are encouraged to enjoy novels, stories, plays, films and poetry – not just to learn about how they are written – and that they have opportunities to listen to, repeat, learn, recite and join in poems for enjoyment. It is also important to encourage children to read non-fiction for enjoyment as well as for finding specific information. Many of the activities can be adapted for use at different levels, to suit the differing levels of attainment of the children (see the Teachers' notes on the pages). Several can be used in different ways as explained in the *Notes on the activities* (see page 6).

## Reading

Most children will be able to carry out the activities independently but a few might need help in reading some of the instructions on the sheets. It is expected that someone will read them to or with them, or explain them, if necessary.

## Organisation

The activities require very few resources besides pencils, crayons, scissors and glue. Other materials are specified in the teachers' notes on the pages: for example, fiction, poetry or information books, websites and CD-ROMs.

## Extension activities

Most of the activity sheets end with a challenge (*Now try this!*) which reinforces and extends the children's learning. These more challenging activities might be appropriate for only a few children; it is not expected that the whole class should complete them, although many more children might benefit from them with appropriate assistance – possibly as a guided or shared activity. On some pages there is space for the children to complete the extension activities, but others will require a notebook or a separate sheet of paper.

## Accompanying CD

The enclosed CD-ROM contains all the activity sheets from the book in a program which allows you to edit them for printing or saving. This means that modifications can be made to further differentiate the activities to suit pupils' needs. See page 14 for further details.

# Notes on the activities

The notes below expand upon those which are provided at the bottom of the activity pages. They give ideas for making the most of the activity sheet, including suggestions for the whole-class introduction, the plenary session or for follow-up work using an adapted version of the sheet. To help teachers to select appropriate learning experiences for their pupils, the activities are grouped into sections but the pages need not be presented in the order in which they appear, unless stated otherwise.

## Stories and poems featured or suggested in this book and supplementary texts

### Novels and stories by significant children's authors

Dick King-Smith: *The Water Horse, The Sheep-Pig, The Jenius, Babe: The Gallant Pig, Dodos Are Forever, The Toby Man, Ace: The Very Important Pig, Martin's Mice, Silver Jackanory, The Cuckoo Child, The Guard Dog, Lightning Strikes Twice, Find the White Horse, Lady Daisy, Super Terrific Pigs, Pretty Polly, The Finger Eater, Harry's Mad, The Merrythought, The Swoose, Uncle Bumpo, Dragon Boy, Horse Pie, The Invisible Dog, Connie and Rollo, Harriet's Hare, Bobby the Bad, Three Terrible Trins, The Clockwork Mouse, King Max, Omnibombulator, Warlock Watson, All Because of Jackson, Dirty Gertie Macintosh, The Stray, Treasure Trove, King Max the Last, Smasher, Winter Wonderland, Clever Duck, What Sadie Saw, The Merman, Mixed-up Max, A Mouse Called Wolf, How Green Was My Mouse, The Robber Boy, Pig in the City, Mr Ape, The Crowstarver, The Witch of Blackberry Bottom, Charlie Muffin's Miracle Mouse, Poppet, The Roundhill, Spider Sparrow, Just in Time, The Magic Carpet Slippers, Julius Caesar's Goat, Mysterious Miss Slade, Lady Lollipop, Billy the Bird, Back to Front Benjy, Fat Lawrence, Funny Frank, Titus Rules!, The Golden Goose, Traffic, Clever Lollipop, The Nine Lives of Aristotle, The Adventurous Snail, Aristotle, Just Binnie, The Catlady, Hairy Hezekiah, Dinosaur Trouble, The Mouse Family Robinson, Ninnyhammer, Twin Giants*

Anne Fine: *Bill's New Frock, How To Write Really Badly, The Summer House Loon, The Other Darker Ned, The Stone Menagerie, Round Behind the Ice-house, The Granny Project, Scaredy-Cat, Anneli the Art Hater, Madame Doubtfire, A Pack of Liars, Crummy Mummy and Me, Goggle-Eyes, The Country Pancake, Stranger Danger?, The Worst Child I Ever Had, The Book of the Banshee, Design A Pram, The Same Old Story Every Year, The Haunting of Pip Parker, The Angel of Nitshill Road, The Chicken Gave It To Me, Flour Babies, Press Play, Step by Wicked Step, Countdown, Jennifer's Diary, The Tulip Touch, Loudmouth Louis, Roll Over Roly, Charm School, Bad Dreams, Notso Hotso, How to Cross the Road and Not Turn Into a Pizza, Up on Cloud Nine, The More the Merrier, Frozen Billy, The True Story of Christmas, Raking the Ashes, It Moved!, On the Summer-House Steps, The Road of Bones, Jamie and Angus Together, Ivan the Terrible, Saving Miss Mirabelle*

### Traditional stories, fables, myths, legends

*Robin Hood* (book & CD, Philip Neil, Dorling Kindersley), *Robin Hood on the Outlaw Trail Again* (Richard Rutherford-Moore, Capall-Bann), *Robin and the Minstrel* (Paul Storrie, Rick Gulick, Steve Bird, Moonstone), *Robin Hood on The Outlaw Trail in Nottingham and Sherwood Forest* (Richard Rutherford-Moore, Capall-Bann), *Castle Diary* (Richard Platt & Chris Riddell, Walker Books); audio books: *Robin Hood: Will You Tolerate This?, Robin Hood: Sheriff got your Tongue?, Robin Hood: Who Shot the Sheriff?, Robin Hood: Parent Hood* (BBC, Icelandic)

### Stories from other cultures

*Parvana's Journey* (Deborah Ellis, OUP), *On the Run* (Elizabeth Laird, Mammoth), *Abdullah's Butterfly* (Janine M. Fraser, HarperCollins), *Grace and Family* (Mary Hoffman, Frances Lincoln), *Tales from Africa* (Mary Medlicott, Kingfisher), *The Barefoot Book of Animal Tales* (Naomi Adler, Barefoot), *Stories from a Shona Childhood* (Charles Mungoshi, Baobab Books), *The Well* (Mildred Taylor, Heinemann)

### Older literature

The *Just William* series (Richmal Crompton, Macmillan), *The Secret Garden* (Frances Hodgson Burnett, Puffin), *Tom's Midnight Garden* (Philippa Pearce, Puffin), *The Borrowers* (Mary Norton, Puffin), *The Jungle Book* (Rudyard Kipling, OUP), *The Railway Children* (Edith Nesbit, Penguin), *Black Beauty* (Anna Sewell, Penguin)

### Useful books of poems

*The Works* (chosen by Paul Cookson, Macmillan)
*The Works 2* (chosen by Brian Moses & Pie Corbett, Macmillan)
*I Like This Poem* (chosen by Kaye Webb, Puffin)
*The Hutchinson Treasury of Children's Poetry* (edited by Alison Sage, Hutchinson)
*The Kingfisher Book of Children's Poetry* (selected by Michael Rosen, Kingfisher)
*The Puffin Book of Twentieth-Century Children's Verse* (edited by Brian Patten, Puffin)
*The Poetry Book: Poems for Children* (chosen by Fiona Waters, Dolphin)
*Read Me: A Poem A Day For The National Year Of Reading* (chosen by Gaby Morgan, Macmillan)
*Read Me 2: A Poem For Every Day of The Year* (chosen by Gaby Morgan, Macmillan)
*Classic Poems to Read Aloud* (selected by James Berry, Kingfisher)
*The Oxford Treasury of Classic Poems* (OUP)
*A Child's Garden of Verses and Underwoods* (Robert Louis Stevenson; first published 1885, more recently by Simon & Schuster)
*Give Yourself a Hug* (Grace Nichols, A & C Black)
*Asana and the Animals: A Book of Pet Poems* (Walker Books)
*Paint Me A Poem: New Poems Inspired by Art in the Tate* (A & C Black)

### Software

*Hot Potatoes* (Half-Baked Software), *Ponds and Streams* (Spiny Software)

## Useful websites

### Narrative

Dual-language books:
http://www.kingston.gov.uk/browse/leisure/libraries/childrens_library_service/dual_language.htm

Selected fiction and non-fiction books and book boxes:
http://www.badger-publishing.co.uk/,
http://www.madeleinelindley.com/aboutus.aspx

Stories from other cultures:
Deborah Ellis: http://www.allenandunwin.com/Authors/
apEllis.asp

War zones:
www.warchild.org.uk
www.christianaid.org.uk/stoppoverty/conflict

Information on Agra, India:
http://en.wikipedia.org/wik/Agra
www.agraindia.org.uk

Myths, fables, legends:
http://home.freeuk.net/elloughton13/theatre.htm
www.mysteriousbritain.co.uk/legends/legendstemplate.html
(Legends of Britain)
http://www.aesopfables.com/ (Fables of Aesop)
www.robinhood.ltd.ukrobinhood/Rutherford_Moore_Reprt.html
(the Robin Hood legend)
www.robinhood.info/keycharacters.html (characters in the Robin
Hood legend)
www.bbc.co.uk/nottingham/360/where_to_go/castle (tour of
Nottingham Castle)
www.channel4.com/history/microsites/H/history/n-s/robin08.html
(Channel 4 history – with links to many Robin Hood sites)
www.robinhood.info (Robin Hood World Wide Society)

Film narrative:
*The Piano* by Aidan Gibbons: for links using IWB software see
the Primary Strategy. The following work without IWB software:
http://www.gutenberg.org/dirs/etext99/rlwyc10.txt,
http://video.google.com/videoplay?docid=
5422822544003533526

### Non-fiction

http://news.bbc.co.uk/cbbcnews/hi/uk/default.stm (a news site
for children)

### Poetry
Poetry to listen to:
http://laurable.com/audio.html
http://www.poets.org/audio.php
http://www.bbc.co.uk/arts/poetry/outloud/

Robert Louis Stevenson:
http://www.nls.uk/rlstevenson/ (biography and links to other
sites)
http://www.poetryloverspage.com/poets/stevenson/stevenson_
ind.html
http://www.bartleby.com/people/StvnsnR.html
http://www.poetryloverspage.com/poets/stevenson/collections/
childs_garden_of_verses.html (poems online)

Grace Nichols:
http://www.contemporarywriters.com/authors/?p=auth79
(biographical and other details)

The book is divided into three main sections: **Narrative**,
**Non-fiction** and **Poetry**. These are sub-divided to match the
Planning Units of the Primary Framework for Literacy.

## Narrative
### *Novels and stories by significant children's authors*

These activities are about stories by contemporary children's
writers, with a focus on Dick King-Smith and the mid-twentieth
century author Richmal Crompton (also featured under *Older
literature*). Other authors to read include: Joan Aiken,
David Almond, Malorie Blackman, Judy Blume, Betsy Byars,
Helen Cresswell, Gillian Cross, Berlie Doherty, Anne Fine,
Michael Foreman, Kevin Crossley-Holland, Penelope Lively,
Michelle Magorian, Margaret Mahy, Michael Morpurgo,
Beverley Naidoo, Terry Pratchett, Philip Pullman,
J. K. Rowling, Robert Westall and Jacqueline Wilson.

**Open a story** and **Start with a question** (pages 15–16) help
the children to experiment with narrative forms and styles to
write their own stories. The children experiment with different
story openings. The activities provide opportunities for the
children to change the order of material within a paragraph and
to consider the effects. You could ask them to compare the
effect if the opening is changed: for example, beginning *The
Water Horse* with *Kirstie found a 'mermaid's purse' just above
the high-tide mark*. Ask them why they think the author preferred
to begin *It was Kirstie who found it*. Similarly, the children could
consider the effect of changing the opening of *The Sheep-Pig*
to *Mrs Hogget heard the very high, very loud, very angry-
sounding squealing of a pig*. Discuss the effect of beginning,
as the author did, with a question. Encourage the children to
discuss and note ideas as they experiment with their story
openings.

**The temptation: 1** and **2** (pages 17–18) encourage the children
to experiment with narrative forms and styles, providing support
to help them to write a new scene for a story. They learn from an
author about how to use narrative to describe the key features
of a scene, to develop a character
and to introduce a key event into
a story. They can also learn
from this passage how to
create tension. Here this is
achieved through William's
thoughts as he reads the
notice, considers what might

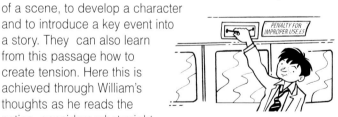

happen if he pulls the communication cord and finally
persuades himself that it will be all right if he pulls it only a little.
The contrasting short sentences recount what happens after
he pulls the cord a little, then a little harder, then much harder.
The children could try using this technique in their 'Temptation'
story. This activity could be linked with work in citizenship on
Choices in which the children focus on the consequences of
choices they make.

**Borrow a character** (page 19) helps the children to work independently to plan (and later, write) a complete story with an interesting story opening, paragraphs for build-up, climax or conflict, resolution and ending. They build their story around a character they have come across in their reading. They could begin by thinking about a character they know from stories, then imagining him or her in a setting they know which is compatible with the character, introducing an event and then considering how this character would respond.

## Traditional stories, myths, fables, legends

This section encourages the children to use what they have learned from their reading of traditional stories to plan and write episodes for legends and folk-tales.

**The rescue plan** (page 20) introduces the setting of the legend of Robin Hood and encourages the children to experiment with the narrative form of the legend in planning their own stories. They should first read the legend of Robin Hood (see page 6 for books and audio books and use the IWB file *Year 5 F legend RH*). They could also explore the setting through the IWB PowerPoint file *Castle Attack* (see Primary Framework for Literacy: Planning, Year 5 Unit 2 Resources; also the Nottingham Castle website www.bbc.co.uk/nottingham/360/where_to_go/castle). It is useful if the children also contribute to a class glossary of castle vocabulary. This could be stored in a table in Word, to allow flexibility in the addition of new head words. These can be added either in their correct alphabetical place by using Insert Row or at the end of the table (using Insert row or the Tab key) and sorted alphabetically by using Sort in the Table menu. A useful reference book is *Castle Diary* by Richard Platt & Chris Riddell (Walker Books). Allow the children time to research the setting – both place and time – before they plan what might happen in the story.

**The rescue: game board** and **The rescue: game cards** (pages 21–22) should be used together to lead to writing in which the children experiment with the narrative form of the legend. The structure of the game board helps the children to plan a story in the form of a legend and, while using this narrative form, to consider details of settings and characters. They could then use a 'story mountain' planning sheet (see page 19) to help them to plan their own episode in the Robin Hood legend. During the game, the children can refer to the legend they know but they are also free to make up some appropriate events if, for example, they land on 'Take a character card and a settings card. Say what important action the character does there.' They could write notes as they go along so they remember the sequence of events and the cards chosen. The children collect or lose points as indicated in the circles on the board. The winner is the one with the most points when all players have reached the story

ending. The children could use the game to help them to create a setting and characters as well as the plot for a story. These could be keyed in and stored as a multi-layered text.

**Legend research** (page 23) provides an opportunity to experiment with the narrative form and style of a legend. The children learn that research is necessary in order to set the historical context of a legend. It could be linked with work in history. The extension activity could be completed by all children, with appropriate support. They should first have listened to someone telling the story and identified the ways in which he or she drew in the reader: for example, through varying tone of voice, volume, pace, facial expression and movement. Link this with work in speaking and listening (Telling a story using storytelling techniques). Ask them to record and play back their introduction and to change it where necessary.

**The hidden folk** (page 24) offers an opportunity to experiment with the narrative form and style of a folk-tale. It presents a traditional Icelandic tale written in an uninteresting way and invites the children to retell it so that it sounds more interesting. They can do this by varying the pace through direct and reported speech, portraying action and selecting detail. There is scope for the children to reflect on their writing and edit and improve it. They could introduce additional dialogue into the story to replace some of the reported speech and add exclamations to express Eve's embarrassment at not having washed all her children before God came to visit. They could also present the consequences of Eve's attempted deception through direct speech. The style of the final sentence should reflect the style of many folk-tales: addressing the reader personally to invite him or her to remember the lesson of the story and to believe its consequences. The children might also find it interesting to read real-life stories of events that have been attributed to 'the hidden folk'. (See also *Icelandic Folk and Fairy Tales* by May & Hallberg Hallmundsson (Iceland Review), *Icelandic Folktales and Legends* by Jacqueline Simpson (Tempus) and websites such as www.isholf.is/gardarj/folk/alar.htm and www.sbac.edu/~media/storytelling_links.htm.)

## Stories from other cultures

Here the children write their own stories that draw on their developing awareness of the ways in which setting and culture affect characters and events. The activities can be linked with work in citizenship on Living in a diverse world and on Children's rights – human rights.

**Asif's viewpoint: 1** and **2** (pages 25–26) draw on the children's reading (*Parvana's Journey* by Deborah Ellis). They experiment with a narrative form that makes significant use of dialogue to tell the story from a different point of view but, as in the original, in the third person. They should focus on how the situation must have appeared to Asif, the boy who was living in the cave. To help, you could ask questions such as *Would Asif have known Parvana's name? How will you change the story to show this? Would Asif have known how Parvana felt?* It is useful to point out that, instead of Parvana trying to find out about the boy in the cave, Asif would have been trying to find out about the girl outside, for example:

> 'Get out of my cave!'
> Asif could hear the girl running away.
> Then silence. She had stopped. Then
> he saw her at the mouth of the cave.
> 'Hello,' she called.
> Asif called back, 'I told you to get out
> of my cave!'

The children could highlight those parts of the extract which in particular show Parvana's viewpoint. This will act as a visual aid as they write their own version.

**War zone research** and **Letter from a war zone** (pages 27–28) help the children to adapt non-narrative forms to help them to write fiction. They find out about a war zone, make notes about the effects the war has on real children and then use their notes to inform narrative writing in the form of a letter. They may find the following websites useful: www.warchild.org.uk and www.christianaid.org.uk/stoppoverty/conflict. It is important to be aware of children in your class and school who may have experienced life in a war zone. The activities require them to consider the appropriate language register for a letter to a pen-friend – informal and personal, using the first person.

**Agra mystery: 1** (page 29) develops the children's skills in researching the setting for a story in a different culture. They adapt non-narrative text to help in writing fiction. Point out that professional fiction writers research and make notes to help them to write in a way that convinces their readers – that research is not only for factual writing.

**Agra mystery: 2** (page 30) focuses on experimenting with a narrative form and using the children's previous non-narrative note-making in order to tell a story. They develop the viewpoint through the use of direct and reported speech, portrayal of action and selection of detail. It is useful to write a sample paragraph as if no research has been done: for example, in which the children are not named and might be playing in a garden when birds fly from a tree (giving no details of what the garden is like, the type of tree, the colours of the birds and so on). Invite the children to develop the description and narrative using the details they found in their research. The children can make their own decision about whether to write a first- or third-person narrative.

## Older literature

> In this section the children use what they have learned from their reading of classic stories to help them to write their own stories in a similar style. They incorporate the patterns of relationships, customs and attitudes from classic stories and use language registers that differ from contemporary stories.

**Just William: 1** and **2** (pages 31–32) present a passage from a story written in the 1950s that invites the children to compare the language of William and his friends with the language they use when talking to their own friends. Allow the children to read and enjoy the text on page 31 before focusing on the language. They should notice expressions that are rarely heard nowadays, such as *foes, ripping, topping, simply topping, I'm frightfully sorry*. To help them to compile the glossary, suggest that they list the words on a jotter first and then put them in alphabetical order. Remind them how to order words that begin with the same letter (or the same two, or even three, letters). In **Just William: 2**, the children read a passage based on a *Just William* story but changed into modern-day English. They are asked to use what they have learned about the language of older stories, and what they know about daily life at the time, to help them to rewrite the paragraph in the style of a *Just William* story.

**Story time** (page 33) invites the children to experiment with a narrative form as they plan their own story on the theme of the passage they read from a *Just William* story (page 31) and using what they have learned from the story (and from other *Just William* stories and other classic children's stories) about children at the time. For some children, setting their writing in their grandparents' childhood might involve a shift of national setting. Stress that the children are to try to replicate the setting of William's adventures (1950s England) rather than the place of their own grandparents' childhood.

## Film narrative

> In these activities the children use what they have learned about the role played by the camera in telling a story, in particular a story told through 'flashbacks', and the way in which a story can be told and emotions communicated without any spoken dialogue. The activities draw on the short (2 minutes) animated film *The Piano* by Aidan Gibbons, which the Primary Strategy recommends for this purpose (see page 7 for useful websites). See also the activities based on this film in *100% New Developing Literacy Understanding and Responding to Texts: Ages 9–10* and *Ages 10–11*. The children will need to watch the film again.

**Is this your life?** (page 34) invites the children to consider the key events in a person's life. They could first identify the key events in the life of the main character in the film *The Piano* by

Aidan Gibbons and consider how these events are presented (through flashback). They experiment with the form of film narrative to plan their own biographical film about someone they know. This could be linked with work in citizenship on Relationships. It also provides an opportunity for speaking and listening as the children prepare and ask questions and listen to the responses.

**Life story** (page 35) provides a structure to help the children to experiment with a different narrative form and style (an animated film without dialogue) to tell a story of their own. Having identified the five key events in a person's life (see page 34), they devise ways of portraying these as 'snapshots', using 'flashback' techniques and mini-dramas. They first need to have watched the film *The Piano* (see above). The images they select to show on the screen could include photographs, greetings cards (for example, bar mitzvah, bat mitzvah, amrit ceremony, new job, new home, wedding, birth congratulations, baptism, naming ceremony, wedding anniversary). They could also include their own drawings based on the key events.

**Biopic** (page 36) provides a structure to help the children to experiment with a different narrative form and style (animated film without dialogue) to write a story of their own. Having interviewed their subject, selected five key events in the person's life and made notes about how to portray these on screen, the children now consider how these will be presented on screen and how they will be linked: for instance, by music (a piano or another instrument). They will need to consider what they have learned about visual and audio techniques and their effects: music, singing, animation, mini-plays, close-ups, panoramic views, camera angle, panning.

**Evaluator** (page 37) develops the children's skills in reflecting independently and critically on their own writing so that they can edit and improve it. Their short film can be a collection of still images (photographs and drawings) linked by music, spoken words  or other devices. They could also create movement through a simple animation either by using special software or by drawing several images with slight differences and showing them in quick succession. They should consider the ways in which colour affects the mood or atmosphere of a scene, the emotions communicated by facial expressions, the ways in which movement can be used to tell a story, indicate the passage of time or communicate feelings, and how sounds can evoke memories, communicate feelings and create an atmosphere. Encourage the children to discuss one another's work – to get input and feedback from other viewers. During the plenary session, ask them for evidence to support their explanations.

## Dramatic conventions

This section combines narrative with non-fiction. It develops the children's awareness that non-fiction, like fiction, has scripts that have to be researched and fosters skills in researching and preparing scripts and presenting information using both fiction and non-fiction writing. The activities presented here have natural links with work in citizenship (Taking part – developing skills of communication and participation; Local democracy for young citizens).

**Leisure survey** and **Leisure documentary planner** (pages 38–39) help the children to research and plan a non-fiction script. You could introduce it though fiction, in the form of a short play in which a group of children complain about how bored they are because there is nothing to do in their locality and then someone (perhaps a teacher, parent or local council representative) asks them if they are sure there really is nothing to do and challenges them to find out. You could ask the class what they know about activities in the locality and how they can find out about them. The audience for the documentary could be other children in the area and other schools. Thinking about the audience will help the children to consider different ways of combining information and style of address, music and so on.

**On screen: 1** and **2** (pages 40–41) encourage the children to adapt narrative and non-narrative forms and styles to write a factual text. They help to scaffold the children's detailed planning and writing of a documentary on leisure facilities in their locality. The task is closely structured but if the children have other ideas about how to make their documentary, they should be encouraged to explore these, too. They begin the activity by writing the script for a mini-play to introduce the theme. This builds on their previous learning about plays and draws on their developing understanding of television scripts (see *100% New Developing Literacy Understanding and Responding to Texts: Ages 9–10*). **On screen: 1** encourages the use of a questioning technique in order to research and present information. When the children evaluate it they should consider how well it makes the audience want to know the information that follows. **On screen: 2** helps the children to make the transition from fiction/drama to non-fiction, factual text. It is useful to remind them of the purpose of a documentary – to present researched facts honestly and in a way that engages the audience's interest. This could include the consideration of bias.

# Non-fiction

## Instructions

This section develops the children's skills in writing instructions. It features activities based on the popular and highly recommended software *Ponds and Streams* (from Spiny Software) and *Hot Potatoes*, which is freely available (for education use) and recommended for this purpose by the Primary Framework. These activities can be adapted for use with other software. There are also generic activities designed to be applied to any software.

**Instruct me** (page 42) develops skills in adapting a narrative form and style to write instructions. For a more demanding activity you could scan the text in the box and alter the order of the narrative sentences so that the children are required to put them in order as well as write them in the imperative form. The children should

follow each other's instructions to see if they work. They could also explore the software before attempting to rewrite the recount. This will reinforce the value of rehearsing the instructions orally first and help to make sense of the use of instructional/imperative language.

**Mixed-up instructions** (page 43) helps the children to adapt a narrative form and style to write instructions and to put the text in the correct order as well as write them in the imperative form. They also experiment with the order of sentences and change the order of material in a paragraph in order to achieve a logical set of instructions. Having played the game, the children could add some tips for users: for example, how to navigate around the pond, what some of the screen icons mean and where to look for some items they need. Stress that the children should bear in mind the potential audience and that the purpose of the activity is to try to make the instructions clear for those who have never played the game before.

**The instructor** (page 44) provides an opportunity for the children to write a factual text with a logical order. They write an instructional text using the appropriate form and features and they could cut out and rearrange the notepads in order to experiment with the order of sentences. Their instructions should take into account the needs of the intended audience.

## Recounts

These activities develop the children's skills in devising questions to find information and making notes from which to write a recount. The activities can be linked with work in citizenship (People who help us – the police and In the media – what's the news?).

**Interviews to recount: 1** and **2** (pages 45–46) develop the children's understanding of the differences between reported and direct speech and writing in paragraphs appropriately, using connectives to improve the flow of their writing. The activities present examples in order to help the children to compose questions that elicit the most information about a

topic and to write a recount. The children learn how to incorporate quotations from eye-witnesses to enliven a recount and demonstrate its reliability. They also learn how to structure a recount to include an introduction to orientate the readers and make them want to read on and a summary to indicate what might happen as a result of the events or to explain something. It is useful if they have first completed the activities in the Recounts section of *100% New Developing Literacy Understanding and Responding to Texts: Ages 9–10*.

**News team** (page 47) provides a format that helps the children to work as a team in researching a topic, collating the research and planning the recount. In doing so they develop speaking and listening skills (Group discussion and interaction). For this activity, ensure that the children follow the school's guidelines for working with adults. They should discuss what they have learned about an incident from different sources. This might involve checking conflicting information in order to present an honest, unbiased recount. They could go on to write the report and submit it to the school magazine or website.

## Persuasive writing

This section develops skills in using language in order to persuade people to do something through appealing to their feelings, common sense, values and aspirations. They also develop skills in the techniques of persuasion: for example, rhetorical questions, sentences in the imperative mood, ambiguity, half-truth, bias and the expression of opinions as if they are facts.

**Ghostly persuasion** (page 48) helps the children to adapt a non-narrative form and style to write a persuasive text. They use persuasive techniques such as opinions presented as facts, half-truth and bias in order to persuade the readers either that ghosts should be allowed to haunt people or that this should be banned. Point out that the same dialogue can be used to support either opinion. The children could also use this page as a starting point for a group or class debate about whether ghosts should be allowed to haunt people. They should read the quotations and then form their own opinion (or you could ask half the class to argue for the ghosts and the other half for the spook police). They can then use the arguments that best suit their purpose. Remind them of useful persuasive phrases such as *surely, clearly,* any *right-thinking person, anyone with any common sense, it stands to reason, no one doubts* and rhetorical questions like *What is the problem? Who could doubt...?* This can be linked with work in speaking and listening (Group discussion and interaction).

**Professor Phake's lecture** (page 49) helps the children to experiment with the order of paragraphs to achieve a persuasive effect. It develops skills in using persuasive language in linking ideas in a persuasive text. Having written Professor Phake's lecture, the children could practise reading it aloud with a friend and then a volunteer

could be invited to present the lecture to the class, who could vote on the question of whether it persuades them that there is life on Mars. Remind them of the importance of tone of voice (and changes in tone, pitch and volume) when they present or evaluate a talk.

**The persuader** (page 50) helps the children to construct an argument in note form to persuade others of a point of view and then to experiment with the order of paragraphs to achieve a persuasive effect and to construct an argument to persuade. It also consolidates letter-writing skills from previous years and encourages the children to group ideas in paragraphs. For a more challenging activity, ask them to write up their notes in a logical order without cutting them out and physically arranging them. This also provides an opportunity to remind them of letter-writing conventions and to discuss the appropriate style of language for this type of letter. It could be linked with work in citizenship (Taking part – developing skills of communication and participation).

**Pigeons: 1** and **2** (pages 51–52) provide an opportunity for the children to adapt persuasive writing for a purpose, to experiment with the order of paragraphs and to present some researched facts to use in a persuasive text. Encourage them to use persuasive devices such as rhetorical questions (for example, *Do you want to be guilty of causing injuries and suffering to pigeons as they fly into sharp wire or become entangled on coils of wire? The town council pays for rubbish left by humans and their dogs to be cleaned up, so what is wrong with cleaning up after pigeons? Are we going to discourage people from coming into the town centre, too?*) Speaking and listening skills are developed as the children plan and present a talk and the others listen and then present counter-arguments, stressing different facts. They should consider how they present the talk: for example, when to look up from the script, making eye contact with the audience, using body language, changing their tone of voice. It can be linked with work in citizenship (Animals and us; Local democracy for young citizens).

## Poetry

### *Poetic style*

Here the children read and respond to poems by contrasting writers and write their own verses in similar styles.

**Build a poem** (page 53) develops from a poem by Robert Louis Stevenson which is featured in *100% New Developing Literacy Understanding and Responding to Texts: Ages 9–10* (page 52). The children should notice the theme of the poem and the regular rhyme pattern; also the use of verbs in the first person to express his interaction with the scene the poet imagines he is building. The children build their own 'Block City' and then describe it in a verse. Allow time for them to 'play with ideas and words' before they begin writing. They can then make a note of the words and phrases they think sound the best. Evaluation is

encouraged in the extension activity so that the children can check their poems for sense, mood and atmosphere as well as the rhyme pattern.

In **Personify it** (page 54) the children explore and develop their understanding of personification before reading a poem that features it (page 55). They should notice that objects and places are described as if they are human and that the nouns and verbs used in these examples are normally associated with the actions of people: *shrugged* off, *stretched* their *arms, darted* its *sharp glances, silently slid, pushing, searching.* There is even an adverb that would normally be associated with humans (*patiently*). Other poems that feature personification include 'Mrs Moon', 'Bully Night', 'The Snowman', 'Your Friend the Sun', 'MARCH ingorders' (Roger McGough, all in *Sky in the Pie*, Puffin), 'Snow on Snow' (Ted Hughes, in *The Puffin Book of Twentieth-Century Children's Verse*), 'Trees in the Moonlight' (James Reeves, in *The Puffin Book of Twentieth-Century Children's Verse*).

**Early morning** (page 55) provides an opportunity for the children to adapt a non-narrative form (poetry) to write their own verse. It presents a poem by Grace Nichols, a contemporary poet from Guyana now living in Britain (see also *100% New Developing Literacy Understanding and Responding to Texts: Ages 9–10* (page 53)). Draw the children's attention to the irregular rhyme pattern (in the first verse the first two lines rhyme; in the second there is no rhyme and in the third verse the second and fourth lines rhyme). Also point out the rhythm, which seems to gather strength as the village wakes up. Also worth noting is the use of onomatopoeia (*clip-clopping, yawn*) and personification (the sun *yawns* and *pushes* darkness out of *her eye* as if rubbing a sleepy eye on awakening). It is useful to prepare for the children's writing beforehand by asking them to notice the place where they live 'waking up' and to make notes and perhaps to take photographs using a digital camera, which could be downloaded and displayed on an interactive whiteboard. Sound recordings could also be made and incorporated into the presentation.

**Free verse** (page 56) develops the children's appreciation of free verse by presenting an example for them to use as a model (see also *100% New Developing Literacy Understanding and Responding to Texts: Ages 9–10* (page 55)) for an activity based on the same poem but which draws the children's attention to the key features of this style). They should notice the lengths of the lines and the rhythm of the poem. The lines are of varying lengths with no regular pattern and the poem reads like a monologue in prose, although it is set out in lines, unlike prose, which is continuous. The powerful images the poem conjures up are created through the dog metaphor. The word *dog* is not used but the children should easily recognise the metaphor from the nouns, verbs and adjectives: (nouns) *leash, eyes, tongue, head, tail, legs*; (verbs) *looked, panting, run, whimpered*; (adjectives) *frightened, confused*. Here they are asked to imagine a much happier scene in which the pen/dog is happy to run free. They could begin by listing words they would normally associate with a dog running around happily: for example, *pant, play, run, rush, scamper*.

## Classic/narrative poems

This section focuses on well-known poems that tell a story. It features 'The Listeners' by Walter de la Mare and includes ideas that can be used with this or with other poems.

**Poetic characters** and **The Traveller's thoughts** (pages 57–58) invite the children to consider the feelings and thoughts of the characters in the narrative poem 'The Listeners' by Walter de la Mare. They could also draw their impressions of the characters and add thought bubbles. The pictures could be scanned and displayed on an interactive whiteboard so that the children can collaborate on the text to key in to the thought bubbles. They could also write a 'stream of consciousness' account of the traveller's and the listeners' thoughts throughout the poem.

**Another traveller** and **Model poem** (pages 59–60) help the children to adapt a poem to write their own poems about a different traveller in a present-day setting. He might arrive one night to meet someone in a deserted spot such as a factory or office on an industrial estate; he might get out of a car and leave the engine running as he calls out to the people he has come to see; he might dismount from a motorbike (like the original traveller, he would be wearing a helmet – the children could mention the colour); or he might arrive by taxi. He might make or receive a call or text message on a mobile phone. Ask them to include words that describe the setting in the same way as Walter de la Mare did: for example, the ground might be hard, concrete, stony, weed-covered; the building might have flat concrete walls, high windows, steel shutters; there might be few leaves but plenty of barbed wire, broken glass, litter, empty cans, syringes. The poem need not rhyme, but if the children want to use rhyme, you could provide a list of useful rhyming words: *scooter/hooter/computer/looter, motorbike/alike, ground/round/around/sound, phone/alone*.

## Choral and performance

The activities in this section help the children to identify the features that make a poem good to listen to and use them in their own writing.

**Adventures of Isabel: 1** and **2** (pages 61–62) help the children to adapt a poem to write their own verse, using a well-known performance poem as a model. They should first have the opportunity to read 'Adventures of Isabel' aloud and to enjoy it. They could emphasise the repeated chorus-like sections by having the entire group read them, with individuals reading other parts.

**Performance poet** (page 63) provides a planning format to help the children to adapt a poem to write their own poem on the same theme, using language to create effects such as humour, excitement and so on. They also consider the structure of the poem: rhyme pattern, length of lines and rhythm. Remind the children that the poem will be written so that it can be performed. Can they remember the characteristics of performance poems, which they will have identified in their previous reading? They should draw on their knowledge of poems such as 'Adventures of Isabel' and others suggested in *100% New Developing Literacy Understanding and Responding to Texts: Ages 9–10*. They can then rehearse, perform, share, evaluate and improve their poems.

**Performance evaluator** (page 64) provides support to help the children to reflect independently and critically on their own writing or that of others and on the performance itself, thus providing a useful speaking and listening activity.

# Using the CD-ROM

The CD-ROM included with this book contains an easy-to-use software program that allows you to print out pages from the book, to view them (e.g. on an interactive whiteboard) or to customise the activities to suit the needs of your pupils.

## Getting started
It's easy to run the software. Simply insert the CD-ROM into your CD drive and the disk should autorun and launch the interface in your web browser.

If the disk does not autorun, open 'My Computer' and select the CD drive, then open the file 'start.html'.

Please note: this CD-ROM is designed for use on a PC. It will also run on most Apple Macintosh computers in Safari however, due to the differences between Mac and PC fonts, you may experience some unavoidable variations in the typography and page layouts of the activity sheets.

## The Menu screen
Four options are available to you from the main menu screen.

The first option takes you to the Activity Sheets screen, where you can choose an activity sheet to edit or print out using Microsoft Word.

(If you do not have the Microsoft Office suite, you might like to consider using OpenOffice instead. This is a multi-platform and multi-lingual office suite, and an 'open-source' project. It is compatible with all other major office suites, and the product is free to download, use and distribute. The homepage for OpenOffice on the Internet is: www.openoffice.org.)

The second option on the main menu screen opens a PDF file of the entire book using Adobe Reader (see below). This format is ideal for printing out copies of the activity sheets or for displaying them, for example on an interactive whiteboard.

The third option allows you to choose a page to edit from a text-only list of the activity sheets, as an alternative to the graphical interface on the Activity Sheets screen.

Adobe Reader is free to download and to use. If it is not already installed on your computer, the fourth link takes you to the download page on the Adobe website.

You can also navigate directly to any of the three screens at any time by using the tabs at the top.

## The Activity Sheets screen
This screen shows thumbnails of all the activity sheets in the book. Rolling the mouse over a thumbnail highlights the page number and also brings up a preview image of the page.

Click on the thumbnail to open a version of the page in Microsoft Word (or an equivalent software program, see above.) The full range of editing tools are available to you here to customise the page to suit the needs of your particular pupils. You can print out copies of the page or save a copy of your edited version onto your computer.

## The Index screen
This is a text-only version of the Activity Sheets screen described above. Choose an activity sheet and click on the 'download' link to open a version of the page in Microsoft Word to edit or print out.

## Technical support
If you have any questions regarding the *100% New Developing Literacy* or *Developing Mathematics* software, please email us at the address below. We will get back to you as quickly as possible.

educationalsales@acblack.com

# Open a story

- **Use the story** opening **as a model for your own story about finding something.**

Think about …   … what is found …   … where …   … who finds it.

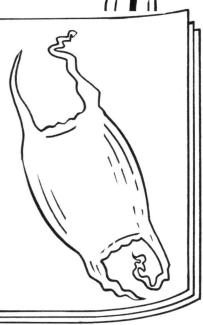

It was Kirstie who found it. It was lying just above the high-tide mark, a squarish package-shaped object, the colour of seaweed, with a long tendril sticking out from each of its four corners.

It was exactly the shape, in fact, of the 'mermaids' purses', the little horny egg capsules of the dogfish, that were commonly washed up on the beach. But this one was the size of a large biscuit tin!

'Look what I've found!' shouted Kirstie. 'Quick, come and look!'

From *The Water Horse* by Dick King-Smith

## Your story

Title _____

It was _____ who found it. It was _____

_____

_____

_____

_____

_____

**NOW TRY THIS!**

- **What happened next?**
- **Plan the story.**

**Teachers' note** Ask the children how the opening invites the reader to read on. What questions does it raise? (for example, *What did Kirstie find? Where? What is special about it?*) You could also discuss how the writer tells readers what a mermaid's purse is and describes it. Ask the children to imagine their story character finding something special – on a beach or in another setting.

100% New Developing Literacy
Creating and Shaping Texts:
Ages 9–10
© A & C BLACK

**15**

# Start with a question

- **Write a story** opening **that starts with a** question .
- **Introduce the main** characters .
- **Describe the** setting .
- **Recount the first event of the story.**

---

'What's that noise?' said Mrs Hogget, sticking her comfortable round red face out of the kitchen window. 'Listen, there 'tis again, did you hear it, what a racket, what a row, anybody'd think someone was being murdered, oh dearie me, whatever is it, just listen to it, will you?'

Farmer Hogget listened. From the usually quiet valley below the farm came a medley of sounds: the oompah oompah of a brass band, the shouts of children, the rattle and thump of a skittle alley, and every now and then a very high, very loud, very angry-sounding squealing lasting perhaps seconds.

Farmer Hogget pulled out an old pocket-watch as big round as a saucer and looked at it. 'Fair starts at two,' he said. 'It's started.'

'I knows that,' said Mrs Hogget, 'because I'm late now with all theseyer cakes and jams, pickles and preserves as is meant to be on the Produce Stall this very minute, and, who's going to take them there, I'd like to know, why you are, but afore you does, what's that noise?'

The squealing sounded again.

From *The Sheep-pig* by Dick King-Smith

---

'_____,' asked _____

| Who asked the question? |

_____

_____

| Describe the character. |

_____

_____

| Where is this? What was going on in the background? |

_____

_____

| What did the other character say and do? |

_____

_____

---

**NOW TRY THIS!**

- **Continue the** dialogue **of your story.**

---

**Teachers' note** Ask the children how the opening invites the reader to read on. What do they want to know? Give them time to imagine another setting in which someone hears (or smells) something and then ask them to model their story opening on the passage – starting with a question and then gradually revealing what is happening.

**100% New Developing Literacy
Creating and Shaping Texts:
Ages 9–10
© A & C BLACK**

**The author describes only the important features of the** setting **.**
- **Underline these.**
- **In a different colour, underline the words that show William's thoughts.**
- Predict **what happens next.**
- **Write** notes **about this.**

Suddenly his eye lit on the notice: "To stop the train, pull down the chain."

William stretched out his hand to it, then read: "Penalty for improper use, £5", and, after a hasty mental calculation that assessed his entire capital at the sum of one shilling and sixpence halfpenny, put his hand down again.

But the fascination of it was more than he could resist. He fingered the chain, and imagined himself pulling it. He wondered if it really worked and, if it worked, how it worked. It probably put on a sort of brake. There wouldn't be any harm in just pulling it a tiny bit. That would only just make the train go a little bit more slowly. No one would even notice it.

He pulled the chain an infinitesimal fraction.

Nothing happened.

He pulled it a little harder.

Still nothing happened.

He pulled it harder still. There was a sudden screaming of brakes, and the train drew to an abrupt standstill. William crouched in his corner of the carriage, frozen with horror. Perhaps, he thought desperately, if he sat quite still and didn't move or breathe, they wouldn't know who'd done it.

From *Sweet William* by Richmal Crompton

**NOW TRY THIS!**
- **Continue the scene.**
- **Write William's thoughts.**
- **Write what William and any other characters said and did.**

**Teachers' note** Ask the children how they felt when reading the passage. Did they want William to pull the communication cord? Did they guess what he would do? Ask them to notice how the author builds up the feeling of tension by recounting William's thoughts and his tentative reaching towards the cord, having second thoughts, then wondering if just a little pull would have just a little effect.

100% New Developing Literacy
Creating and Shaping Texts:
Ages 9–10
© A & C BLACK

**17**

# The temptation: 2

- **Write your own 'temptation' story** boxed[chapter].
- **Use the passage from *Sweet William* as a model.**

## Chapter plan

Character _____

_____

Setting _____

_____

Temptation _____

_____

What the character does _____

_____

_____

_____

_____

_____

> What does the character notice?

_____

_____

> Write a paragraph. Give information about the character and setting.

_____

_____

_____

> What goes through the character's mind?

_____

_____

_____

> Write a paragraph about the character's discussion with himself or herself.

_____

_____

_____

> What does he or she do? What happens?

Continue on the back of the sheet if you need to.

**NOW TRY THIS!**

- **Write a chapter about the** boxed[consequences] **of the temptation.**

**Teachers' note** The children could first talk to a friend about a situation in which they were tempted to do something they knew they should not. They could write their thoughts in speech bubbles. What did they do? What happened – or what might have happened if they had given in to the temptation? Ask them to record these in direct speech to create a feeling of tension.

**100% New Developing Literacy Creating and Shaping Texts: Ages 9–10**
© A & C BLACK

# Borrow a character

- **Plan a story about a** [character] **from a story you have read.**

Character's name _____

Story/stories _____

Author _____

**Opening**
What is the character doing?
Where?
What does the reader need to know about any past events?

**Something happens**
What happens?
What problems does it cause?

**Climax**
What happens to build up the tension, mystery or excitement?

**Resolution**
What happens to solve the problem or mystery?

**Ending**
How are all the events in the story linked to one another?
What happens to the main character and any others?

**NOW TRY THIS!**

Think about what you know about the character.

- **Write the first** [chapter] **of your story.**
- **Give it to a friend to** [edit].

---

**Teachers' note** Use this to develop a story about any fictional character the children like. They can use their knowledge of the character to help them to imagine what he or she might do in a particular situation. You could present them with a situation: for example, seeing someone robbed, finding something valuable or overhearing a conversation that makes him or her want to find out more.

**100% New Developing Literacy
Creating and Shaping Texts:
Ages 9–10**
© A & C BLACK

# The rescue plan

Robin Hood and Will Scarlett are in the woods.

- **How can they rescue Maid Marian from the castle?**
- **Write** notes **about what might happen in each place.**

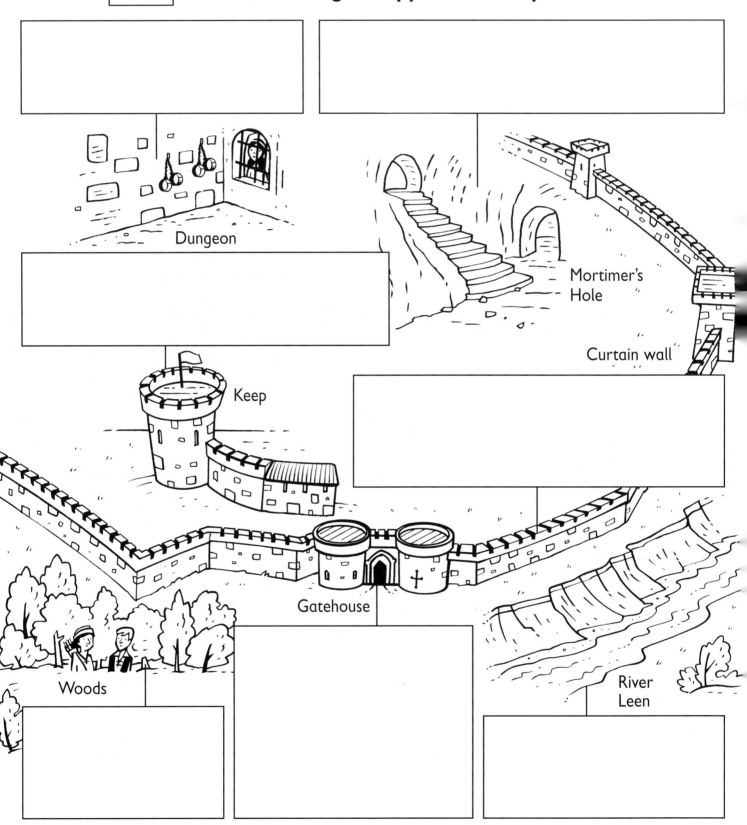

Dungeon

Mortimer's Hole

Curtain wall

Keep

Gatehouse

Woods

River Leen

**Teachers' note** The children first need to have read the legend of Robin Hood (see *Notes on the activities*, page 6). It is also useful if they have looked at the software *Castle Attack* (see page 8). They can then make notes about the problems Robin Hood and Will Scarlett might face as they try to rescue Maid Marian.

**100% New Developing Literacy Creating and Shaping Texts: Ages 9–10**
© A & C BLACK

# The rescue: game board

**Opening**

+2 In two sentences, describe the historical setting.

+1 In one sentence, say what happened before this story began.

Go back two. −1

+3 Take a character card. Give three details about him or her.

+3 Take a character card. Describe the character's personal qualities.

Go back six. −1

Take a settings card. Describe the setting. +3

Go back three. −1

+3 Take a settings card. Say why the setting is important.

Go back two. −1

Take a character card. Give three sentences about the character's life so far. +3

+2 Take a settings card. Describe the atmosphere here.

Go back three. −1

Go back one. −1

+2 Take a character card. Describe a problem he or she faces.

+2 Take a character card. Recount one action by this character.

Describe the main problem faced by the key character. +3

Go back two. −1

Go back three. −1

**Ending**

+4 Take a character card. Say how this character resolves a problem.

+4 Take a settings card. Say how this place is important in resolving a problem.

Go back one. −1

Take a character card and a settings card. Say what important action the character does there. +4

**Teachers' note** The children should first have completed page 20. Use this with the cards on page 22. It is a game for four. Players place a counter on Opening and take turns to roll a die to see how many squares to move. Different squares tell them to talk about parts of the story setting or the characters. They must land on Ending to finish. They then plan a story based on the settings and characters.

**100% New Developing Literacy Creating and Shaping Texts: Ages 9–10 © A & C BLACK**

## Setting cards

A chapel in the castle wall

A dungeon

The gatehouse

Mortimer's Hole

The ramparts along the curtain wall

The keep

## Character cards

Robin Hood, a yeoman who became an outlaw and robbed the rich to help the poor

Maid Marian, a noblewoman and Robin's sweetheart

Will Scarlett, a kinsman of Robin Hood and his faithful supporter

Little John, Robin's right-hand man. A big man and a strong fighter

The Sheriff of Nottingham, who wanted Robin captured

Alan A'Dale, a minstrel and one of the outlaws

**22**

**Teachers' note** The children should first have completed page 20. Cut out the two sets of cards and place them face down in two piles. Use them with the game board on page 21. Players pick up a setting or character card as directed. Once read, these are placed at the bottom of the pile. The children then plan a story based on the settings and characters. Page 23 will help.

**100% New Developing Literacy
Creating and Shaping Texts:
Ages 9–10**
© A & C BLACK

# Legend research

- **Research** the historical setting of a **legend**.
- **Find out about life at the time.**
- **Find out about key people and events of the time.**

## The setting

Make notes about the place.

## Life at the time

## Real historical characters in the legend

Describe the characters. Note their important actions.

### Time-line

| Key events in the legend | Key events in history | Year |
|---|---|---|
| | | |
| | | |
| | | |
| | | |

**NOW TRY THIS!**

- **Write an** introduction **to the legend.**
- **Read this aloud to interest the audience.**

Record the introduction.

**Teachers' note** This could be linked with work in history. The children could research a period they already know something about and then model their legend on the style of others they have read. Point out that authors always research the historical settings of their stories to help them to write accurately and make the stories convincing.

100% New Developing Literacy
**Creating and Shaping Texts:**
**Ages 9–10**
© A & C BLACK

# The hidden folk

- **Rewrite the story.**
- **Make it more interesting for the reader.**

> Use direct speech.
> Use connectives.
> Describe some details.

### The Hidden People
*A folk-tale from Iceland*

Once upon a time, God came to visit Adam and Eve. They received him with joy and showed him everything in their house. Then they showed him their children. God said they were very promising and full of hope. He asked Eve whether she had any other children. She said she had none.

But Eve had not finished washing the children and was ashamed to let God see any dirty, so she had hidden the unwashed ones. God knew this, of course, and said, "What humans hide from God, God will hide from humanity."

So the unwashed children became invisible. They went to live in mounds and hills. The elves are descended from them, but humans come from the children Eve had shown to God. Elves can only be seen by humans if the elves want to be seen.

> What did the characters say? What did the children do?
>
> How did Eve look?

> Link how Eve looked to the other paragraphs. Use connectives. Describe where the elves live. Address the last sentence to the reader using 'you'.

Continue on the back of the sheet if you need to.

**NOW TRY THIS!**

- **Reread your version of the** ⬚legend⬚ .
- ⬚Edit⬚ **it and see if you can improve it.**

---

**Teachers' note** Read the folk-tale to the children and ask them if they enjoyed it. Discuss what would make it more interesting and enjoyable for the reader. Model how to improve the first three or four sentences (see *Notes on the activities*, page 8). Remind them of the rules for writing direct and reported speech.

**24**

**100% New Developing Literacy
Creating and Shaping Texts:
Ages 9–10**
© A & C BLACK

The story is set during a war in Afghanistan.

During the fighting Parvana and her father were separated from her mother and sister. Then her father died. Now Parvana is travelling across the country to find her mother and sister. She is carrying a baby boy she found in a burnt-out house.

Parvana has just come across a cave, which she thinks would be a good place to shelter.

"Get out of my cave!"

Parvana spun around and was running away before the voice stopped echoing off the cave walls. Fear kept her legs moving long after she was exhausted. When she finally slowed down, her brain began to tell her something she had been too scared to hear moments earlier. The voice that had yelled at her from the back of the cave was a child's voice.

Parvana stopped running and caught her breath. She turned around and looked back at the cave. She wasn't going to let some child keep her from getting a few days of rest!

"Let's go and see who's in there," she said to Hassan.

She went back to the mouth of the cave.

"Hello," she called in.

"I told you to get out of my cave!" the voice shouted. It was definitely a child's voice.

"How do I know it's your cave?" Parvana asked.

"I've got a gun. Go away or I'll shoot you."

Parvana hesitated. Lots of young boys in Afghanistan did have guns. But if he had a gun, why hadn't he shot at her already? "I don't believe you," Parvana said. "I don't think you're a killer. I think you're a kid just like me."

She took a few more steps forward, trying to see in the dark. A stone hit her on the shoulder.

"Stop that!" she shouted. "I'm carrying a baby."

"I warned you to stay away."

"All right, you win," Parvana said. "Hassan and I will leave you alone. We just thought you'd like to share our meal, but I guess you'd rather throw stones."

There was a moment's silence.

"Leave the food and go."

"I have to cook it first," Parvana said over her shoulder as she walked away. "If you want it, come out and get it."

Parvana put down the baby where she could watch him and kept talking while she gathered dried grasses and stalks from dead weeds for a cook fire. The water in the stream was clear and moving swiftly, so she thought it would be safe to drink without boiling it first. She dipped in her pan. "Here's some lovely cool water to drink, Hassan," she said. "Tastes good, doesn't it? Drink it all down, and we'll have a hot tasty supper." She gave him a piece of stale naan to keep him quiet until the meal was ready.

Parvana heard a little shuffling noise. Out of the corner of her eye she saw a small boy peering out from the cave. He was sitting on the ground. She took him some water.

**Teachers' note** The children should read this page and then, using page 26 to help, rewrite it from Asif's point of view. Help them to notice the clues that it is written from Parvana's point of view: it expresses her thoughts and what she notices and is based on what she knows and does not know (for example, she does not know who is in the cave and tries to find out).

*100% New Developing Literacy*
**Creating and Shaping Texts:**
**Ages 9–10**
© A & C BLACK

- **Rewrite the passage from *Parvana's Journey* from Asif's** point of view . **The first paragraph has been done for you.**

---

"Get out of my cave!"

Asif smiled to himself. He had scared the girl who had the cheek to come into his cave. She was running away before his voice stopped echoing off the cave walls. She slowed down, looking exhausted.

_____

_____

> Show Asif's thoughts and feelings, but not Parvana's.

_____

_____

_____

_____

> Think about what Asif knows but Parvana does not.

_____

_____

_____

_____

> Think about what Parvana knows but Asif does not.

_____

_____

_____

_____

Continue on the back of the sheet if you need to.

---

**NOW TRY THIS!**

- **Reread what you have written.**
- **Have you shown why the boy was so unfriendly towards Parvana?**
- Edit **and improve your story.**

---

**Teachers' note** Use this with page 25. Having identified the clues that the passage was written from Parvana's point of view, the children can then consider how to alter it so that it represents Asif's point of view: expressing his thoughts and what he notices and basing it on what he knows (for example, he does not know who is outside the cave).

100% New Developing Literacy
Creating and Shaping Texts:
Ages 9–10
© A & C BLACK

# War zone research

- **Use this page to prepare for writing a** $\boxed{\text{story}}$ **set in a war zone.**
- **Find out about life for children who live there.**
- **Write** $\boxed{\text{notes}}$ **.**

Use the Internet.

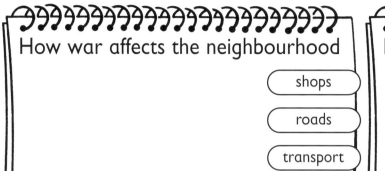

How war affects the neighbourhood

- shops
- roads
- transport

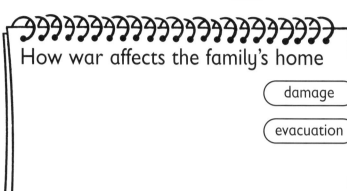

How war affects the family's home

- damage
- evacuation

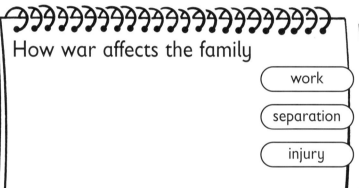

How war affects the family

- work
- separation
- injury

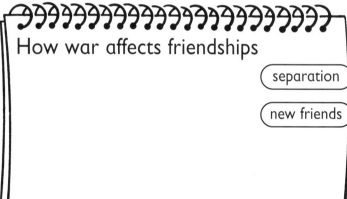

How war affects friendships

- separation
- new friends

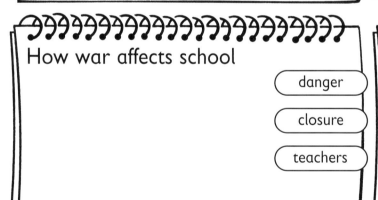

How war affects school

- danger
- closure
- teachers

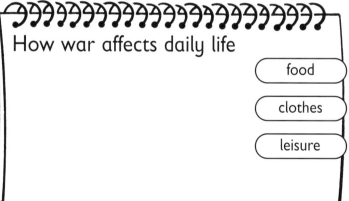

How war affects daily life

- food
- clothes
- leisure

**NOW TRY THIS!**

- **Write three questions you would like to ask a child who lives in a war zone.**

**Teachers' note** The children should first have completed pages 25 and 26, which depict a war zone (Afghanistan). Different children or different groups could research each aspect of the war zone, using the Internet sources suggested in *Notes on the activities* (see page 9) or others. Point out that authors need to find out about setting and culture in order to write a convincing story.

**100% New Developing Literacy
Creating and Shaping Texts:
Ages 9–10**
© A & C BLACK

# Letter from a war zone

- **Write a** letter **from a child in a war zone to tell a pen-friend what has been happening there.**
- **Write in the** first person.

> Use your research about war zones to help.

Your address _____

_____

_____

Date _____

Dear _____

When I woke up this morning _____

_____

_____

_____

_____

_____

_____

_____

_____

> Say how war has affected the child's neighbourhood, family, friends, home, school and daily life.

I hope _____

Best wishes from your friend

_____

**NOW TRY THIS!**

- **Write a reply to the letter.**
- **Ask some questions about it.**

**Teachers' note** Having researched a war zone, the children use the information they have found to support their writing – imagining they are a child living in a war zone who is writing about his or her experiences.

**100% New Developing Literacy
Creating and Shaping Texts:
Ages 9–10**
© A & C BLACK

# Agra mystery: 1

- **Plan a story about a character who goes to Agra, in India, for a holiday.**
- **Make** notes **about what you need to know.**

The Taj Mahal is in Agra

A map of India

The character makes friends with Nimesh and Meena, a brother and sister who live in Agra. The opening of one chapter has been planned for you.

| Story plan | What I need to know |
|---|---|
| Opening | |
| Something happens<br>Character playing in courtyard of Nimesh and Meena's house. Look up as 6 green parrots (rose-ringed parakeets) suddenly squawk and fly out of cypress tree. What had scared them? Boy hiding in tree. | What are houses like in Agra? What kinds of tree grow there? What do they look and smell like? What kinds of bird live in the city? What do they look like? Where might you see them? |
| A problem develops | |
| The problem is resolved | |
| Ending | |

**NOW TRY THIS!**
- **Do the research for your story.**
- **Make notes.**

Useful websites:
http://en.wikipedia.org/wiki/Agra
www.agraindia.org.uk

**Teachers' note** Copy this onto A3 paper. Ask the children what they know about Agra. Tell them the history of the Taj Mahal. Point out the map and ask them to find Agra on a map in an atlas. They could make notes about anything they find out. Tell them they are going to plan a story set in Agra and they need to research this setting. Remind them how to make notes quickly.

100% New Developing Literacy
Creating and Shaping Texts:
Ages 9–10
© A & C BLACK

# Agra mystery: 2

- **Write a paragraph for your story set in Agra, India.**
- **Base it on the notes.**
- **Use your research to help with details.**

_____

_____

Give the main character a name.

_____

_____

Say what the children are playing.

_____

_____

_____

Write some dialogue as well as narrative.

_____

_____

_____

Use interesting vocabulary to help readers to imagine the setting.

_____

**NOW TRY THIS!**

- **Write the opening paragraph of the story, which comes before the one on this page.**
- **Say how the main character got to know Nimesh and Meena.**

**Teachers' note** The children should first have completed page 29. Remind them that some research notes had been filled in for them on page 29 and are repeated here, and model how to fill out the notes into a story passage.

**100% New Developing Literacy
Creating and Shaping Texts:
Ages 9–10**
© A & C BLACK

# Just William: 1

- **Underline any words or phrases which tell you that the passage is from quite an old story.**
- **In a different colour, underline any words or phrases you need to look up in a dictionary.**
- **List these in the** `glossary` **and write their meanings.**

*William Brown and Hubert Lane lead gangs of boys who are always fighting one another. To encourage them to make friends, Mrs Brown invites Hubert and his friends to William's party.*

William did not reply to this because there wasn't anything that he could trust himself to say. He was still restraining himself with great difficulty from hurling himself upon his foes. They went in to tea.

"Oh, I say, how ripping! How topping," said the Hubert Laneites gushingly to Mrs Brown, nudging each other and sniggering whenever her eye was turned away from them. Once Hubert looked at William and made his most challenging grimace, turning immediately to Mrs Brown to say with an ingratiating smile, "It's a simply topping party, Mrs Brown, and it's awfully nice of you to ask us."

Mrs Brown beamed at him and said, "It's so nice to have you, Hubert," and the other Hubert Laneites sniggered, and William kept his hands in his pockets with such violence that one of them went right through the lining.

But the crowning catastrophe happened when they pulled the crackers.

Hubert went up to William, and said, "See what I've got out of a cracker, William" and held up a ring that sent a squirt of water into William's face. The Hubert Laneites went into paroxysms of silent laughter. Hubert was all smirking contrition.

"I say, I'm so sorry, William, I'd no idea that it would do that. I'm frightfully sorry, Mrs Brown. I'd no idea that it would do that. I just got it out of one of the crackers. I say, I'm so sorry, William."

It was evident to everyone but Mrs Brown that the ring had not come out of a cracker, but had been carefully brought by Hubert in order to play this trick on William.

## Glossary

|  |  |
|---|---|
|  |  |
|  |  |
|  |  |
|  |  |
|  |  |
|  |  |

Continue on another piece of paper or key in your glossary.

**NOW TRY THIS!**

- **Rewrite the passage in the type of English you would use.**

**Teachers' note** Read the passage then ask the children what they can tell about the time setting of the story. Which words tell them it is from an older story? They might also notice that the language is more formal than that of most modern stories. It includes some long and quite difficult words that they might need to look up. They should enter these in the glossary in alphabetical order.

**100% New Developing Literacy Creating and Shaping Texts: Ages 9–10**
© A & C BLACK

# Just William: 2

- **Rewrite the passage so that it could belong in a *Just William* story.**
- **Make it sound more** old-fashioned .

Think about old and modern language.

Think about new inventions.

### Waiting for Christmas

"What are you getting for Christmas?" asked William.

"Some sound things from my dad," said Ginger, "like an MP3 player and a new mobile. They're wicked. But my auntie's knitted me a sad green jumper and I know my mum's going to make me wear it. I should be grateful but I'll look such a loser."

William and Ginger usually spent the week before Christmas poking around in cupboards and drawers. They always found the presents their families had hidden.

"I found a load of stuff in the cupboard under the stairs," said William. "I'm getting a new mobile, too, and there's a wicked pair of trainers."

"Nothing to make you cringe?" asked Ginger.

"Yeah – a woolly hat with a bobble. Why do aunties knit things?" replied William.

"I dunno," said Ginger, "They could just cut out the middle man and give us the money. But I can't complain. I've only got £6.50, so I can't buy them anything cool."

"We could make pressies," suggested William, "like sweets. My mum's got loads of cookery books and all the stuff's in the kitchen. We could do it while she's in town tomorrow."

"Sound," said Ginger. "See you then."

---

---

---

---

---

---

---

**NOW TRY THIS!**

- **Write the next paragraph in the same old-fashioned style.**

**Teachers' note** The children need to have read some *Just William* stories so that they are familiar with the setting and the author's style. This passage is based on a *Just William* story but is written as if in the present day. Discuss how they can tell. Ask them about the differences between modern language and the language used in *Just William*. Draw out differences in vocabulary and formality.

**100% New Developing Literacy Creating and Shaping Texts: Ages 9–10**
© A & C BLACK

# Story time

- **Plan a story about a birthday when something went wrong.**
- **The** setting **is when your grandparents were children.**
- **Make** notes **about what you need to find out.**

## Story plan

Opening

Something happens

A problem develops

Climax

Resolution

Ending

## Notes

**NOW TRY THIS!**

- **Do some** research **to find out what you need to know for your story.**

Read novels from the time.

Talk to grandparents or other older people.

**Teachers' note** This follows the theme of the *Just William* story (page 31). Ask the children to make notes about details of a party they have been to and then to introduce an unexpected event or accident and to imagine what might happen as a result. Encourage them to use these notes to write a story that is set in the 1950s. What will be the same, and what different?

**100% New Developing Literacy**
**Creating and Shaping Texts:**
**Ages 9–10**
© A & C BLACK

# Is this your life?

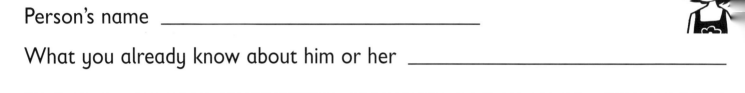

- **Write questions to** [interview] **an older person you know about his or her life story.**
- **Write the answers.**

> Find out about important events in the person's life. Find out about happy and sad memories.

Person's name _____

What you already know about him or her _____

_____

_____

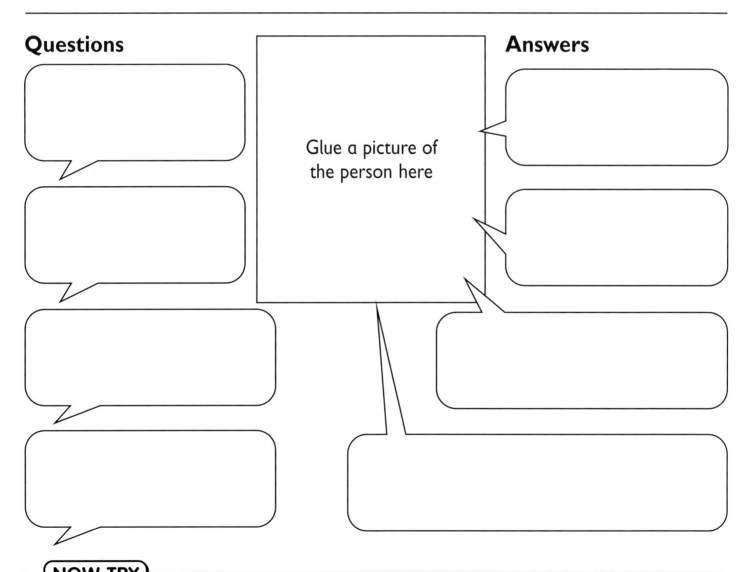

**Questions**

**Answers**

Glue a picture of the person here

**NOW TRY THIS!**

- **Talk to a friend about how you could show this person's life in a** [film] **like *The Piano*.**

**Teachers' note** This could be used for homework. The children will plan a 'life story' film (like *The Piano* – see *Notes on the activities*, pages 9–10, and *100% New Developing Literacy Understanding and Responding to Texts: Ages 9–10*). The subject will be an older person they know. In class they could make notes on what they already know about the person and what they want to find out.

**100% New Developing Literacy Creating and Shaping Texts: Ages 9–10**
© A & C BLACK

# Life story

- **Plan a** ⃞film⃞ **about the life of an older person you know.**
- **Include five key events in the person's life.**
- **Make** ⃞notes⃞ **about what to show on the screen.**

> Use *The Piano* as a model. The film can have music but no dialogue.

| Key event | What you will show on the screen |
|---|---|
| 1 | |
| 2 | |
| 3 | |
| 4 | |
| 5 | |

**NOW TRY THIS!**

- **Collect copies of photographs and other useful pictures to help: for example, important greetings cards, invitations and certificates.**

**Teachers' note** The children should first have completed page 34. Ask them to read their notes and the interview notes and to pick out the five most important events in the person's life. How will they show these on screen as if in a film modelled on *The Piano*? They could watch *The Piano* again and notice how the subject's life story events are presented. See also page 36.

**100% New Developing Literacy
Creating and Shaping Texts:
Ages 9–10**
© A & C BLACK

# Biopic

- Describe the five main scenes in your 'life story' film.
- Show how you will link the scenes.

**Scene 1**

Link

**Scene 2**

Link

**Scene 3**

Link

**Scene 4**

Link

**Scene 5**

Film title _____

Subject _____

Music _____

Why I chose it _____

Links can be people coming and going, the subject's thoughts, important objects and so on.

**NOW TRY THIS!**

- Write Scene 1 in detail. Show how it links to Scene 2.

You could make a labelled sketch.

100% New Developing Literacy
Creating and Shaping Texts:
Ages 9–10
© A & C BLACK

**Teachers' note** The children should first have completed page 34. Use this with page 35. They could first make notes about the images used in *The Piano* to depict key moments in the man's life and how these were linked (music, background changes, colour, costume changes). They should write notes in the boxes about the images they will show and write in the arrows how these will be linked.

# Evaluator

- **Colour the stars to show how well each** `effect` **in your 'life story' film worked.**

- **Explain your** `evaluation` .

| Scene number and description | Effects | Evaluation: Not ⟶ Very effective | Explanation |
|---|---|---|---|
| **1** | Colour | ☆ ☆ ☆ ☆ ☆ | |
| | Facial expressions | ☆ ☆ ☆ ☆ ☆ | |
| | Movement | ☆ ☆ ☆ ☆ ☆ | |
| | Sound | ☆ ☆ ☆ ☆ ☆ | |
| **2** | Colour | ☆ ☆ ☆ ☆ ☆ | |
| | Facial expressions | ☆ ☆ ☆ ☆ ☆ | |
| | Movement | ☆ ☆ ☆ ☆ ☆ | |
| | Sound | ☆ ☆ ☆ ☆ ☆ | |
| **3** | Colour | ☆ ☆ ☆ ☆ ☆ | |
| | Facial expressions | ☆ ☆ ☆ ☆ ☆ | |
| | Movement | ☆ ☆ ☆ ☆ ☆ | |
| | Sound | ☆ ☆ ☆ ☆ ☆ | |
| **4** | Colour | ☆ ☆ ☆ ☆ ☆ | |
| | Facial expressions | ☆ ☆ ☆ ☆ ☆ | |
| | Movement | ☆ ☆ ☆ ☆ ☆ | |
| | Sound | ☆ ☆ ☆ ☆ ☆ | |

**NOW TRY THIS!**

- **Which is the best** `scene` **of your film?**
- **How could you improve one other scene?**

**Teachers' note** Use this page after the children have made a short film of someone's life story. If their film has more than four scenes, provide a second copy of the page with the scene numbers masked. You may wish to enlarge the copies to A3 size to allow more room for the children's explanations of their evaluation scores.

**100% New Developing Literacy Creating and Shaping Texts: Ages 9–10** © A & C BLACK

**37**

# Leisure survey

- **What is there to do in your locality after school and at weekends?**
- **Find out, so that you can plan a** | documentary | **about it.**
- **Make a note of each activity.**

Check in local newspapers.

Ask at leisure centres.

 Ask others in the class what they know.

Ask other children.

Check notices and leaflets in the library.

Check the local council's website.

| Sports | Creative (art, craft, dance, drama) | Entertainment (cinema, theatre, etc.) |
|---|---|---|
| | | |

| Social (clubs for various activities) | Outdoor activities (nature, history, geography) | Other (e.g. Scouts) |
|---|---|---|
| | | |

**NOW TRY THIS!**

- **What do you need to find out about each activity?**
- **Think about the information users will need.**

**Teachers' note** Introduce this activity with a short play (see *Notes on the activities*, page 10). Tell the children that they are going to prepare a short documentary about children's leisure facilities in their area. This can begin with a similar mini-play. Do they think there are many facilities? Ask them what they know about the different categories. They could share the task of finding out within their group.

**100% New Developing Literacy
Creating and Shaping Texts:
Ages 9–10**
© A & C BLACK

# Leisure documentary planner

- Collect information for a documentary about children's leisure activities in your locality.

Your group will research one type of activity.

- Contact the organisers by telephone, text or email.
- Write notes ✓.

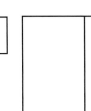
Read advertisements and announcements in local newspapers.

Read notices and leaflets in the library.

Check the local council's website.

**Types of activity**

| ☐ Sports | ☐ Creative | ☐ Entertainment | ☐ Social | ☐ Outdoor | ☐ Other (describe) _____ |

| Activities found | Who can take part (girls, boys, ages, disability access) | When | Where | Cost |
|---|---|---|---|---|
| | | | | |
| | | | | |
| | | | | |

**NOW TRY THIS!**

- How can you present this information in a documentary on screen?
- Think about pictures, photographs, videos, illustrations, maps and diagrams.

---

**Teachers' note** Copy this onto A3 paper. The children should first have completed page 38 and watched and discussed some television documentaries (see *100% New Developing Literacy Understanding and Responding to Texts: Ages 9–10*). Groups should use this to record detailed information about each activity to help them to plan a documentary for video recording.

**100% New Developing Literacy**
**Creating and Shaping Texts:**
**Ages 9–10**
© A & C BLACK

**39**

# On screen: 1

- **Plan a short** play **to introduce your** documentary **about leisure activities.**
- **Begin with two bored children.**
- **Then bring in their parents.**

Work in a group.

What might the bored children say?

What might their parents say?

Think about facial expressions.

Think about actions and body language.

## List of characters

| Name | Description | Name | Description |
|------|-------------|------|-------------|
|  |  |  |  |
|  |  |  |  |

## Dialogue

| Speaker | Stage directions | Spoken words |
|---------|------------------|--------------|
|  |  |  |
|  |  |  |
|  |  |  |
|  |  |  |
|  |  |  |
|  |  |  |
|  |  |  |
|  |  |  |

**NOW TRY THIS!**

- **Act the play with someone watching.**
- Edit **the script.**

How does it look and sound to the audience?

**Teachers' note** The children should first have completed pages 38–39. They can then work in groups to write the script for a mini-play as an introduction to their documentary. They could first enact a scenario in which some bored children are complaining about having nothing to do or are in trouble for anti-social behaviour which they say arose through boredom. Continued on page 41.

**100% New Developing Literacy
Creating and Shaping Texts:
Ages 9–10**
© A & C BLACK

# On screen: 2

- **Link the** play **to the** documentary **that will follow it.**

> Think about what the play was saying and what you found out for your documentary.

## One of the characters could speak to camera.
- **What could he or she say?**

Scene location _____

| Character | On screen<br>Will the character be with the others from the play? Will he or she move away from them? How can you make the others 'disappear'? | Spoken words |
|-----------|------------------------------|--------------|
|           |                              |              |

## Then a reporter could come on screen to introduce the documentary.

> Change the background setting to introduce the leisure activities.

Scene location at start _____

Changes in background/location _____

| Reporter | On screen<br>Will the reporter stand still or walk towards something or someone? | Spoken words |
|----------|------------------------------|--------------|
|          |                              |              |

**NOW TRY THIS!**
- **Video your introduction.**
- **Play it and make** notes **about how to improve it.**

**Teachers' note** The children should first have completed pages 38–40. They could take turns to video record their first attempt and then replay it and edit it to produce a polished performance. They can then plan the factual part of the documentary, with different groups collaborating to produce a report about different types of activity.

**100% New Developing Literacy Creating and Shaping Texts: Ages 9–10**
© A & C BLACK

# Instruct me

- **Read the** recount **that tells how someone used a computer program.**
- **Rewrite it as** instructions **to tell someone how to use the program.**

I put the CD-ROM *Ponds and Streams* into the CD-ROM drive.
When it had loaded, I waited for it to finish the introduction.
Then I clicked on 'Visit the pond'. This started a pond game.
I had to explore the pond and complete all the tasks the pond animals gave me.
I clicked on 'Start new game'. I keyed in my name and clicked OK. A pond came on the screen.
I moved the cursor around the edges of the screen. If an arrow showed, I clicked on it to move right, left, up or down around the pond.
When an animal appeared I clicked on it. This displayed an information box about the animal.
To get rid of the box I clicked on it.
Sometimes a box appeared that gave me a task to complete.
After I had read these I had to click OK to get rid of them.
Each time I completed a task I scored points.
I could end the game at any time by clicking 'End game'.

## How to Play the Pond Game

1  Put the CD-ROM 'Ponds and Streams' into the CD-ROM drive.

2  When it has loaded,

3  _____

4  _____

5  _____

6  _____

7  _____

8  _____

9  _____

10 _____

**NOW TRY THIS!**

- **What else would you like to know?**
- **Write three questions.**

**Teachers' note** Copy this onto A3 paper. Ask the children to read the passage and to identify the features that show it is a recount (past tense, written in the order in which events happened, time connectives such as *Then*). Ask them which words they will change, and how, in order to convert it into instructions. For a more challenging activity the completed example could be masked.

**100% New Developing Literacy
Creating and Shaping Texts:
Ages 9–10**
© A & C BLACK

# Mixed-up instructions

- **Write** | instructions | **for the Pond game tasks. The children's recounts are not in the correct order, so you will need to sort them out.**

> We did this by dragging each bit of litter we found into the backpack. We cleared the litter from the pond. We found the backpack at the bottom left of the screen.

> We had to continue until she was covered. We did this by dragging bits and pieces such as leaves and sticks onto her. We helped Kitty Caddis to make a new case.

> We clicked on each pond animal to find out which one had the lens. First we looked around the pond until we heard the Cyclops say Hello. Once we had found the lens we dragged it onto the backpack icon and clicked on the lens. Then we could see the Cyclops. The Cyclops was too small to see so we had to look for an old spectacle lens to help.

## Clear the pond of litter

_____

_____

## Help Kitty Caddis to make a new case

_____

_____

## Look for the Cyclops

_____

_____

_____

_____

**NOW TRY THIS!**

- **List any words you think should be in the** | glossary |.
- **Write** | definitions | **for them.**

**Teachers' note** Each speech bubble presents a recount of a task within the Pond game. The children need not have used the software, since the focus is on the language and structure of instructions. Ask them to identify the sentence that should come first in each recount. They should notice that the other sentences do not make sense unless they follow this 'topic sentence'.

100% New Developing Literacy
Creating and Shaping Texts:
Ages 9–10
© A & C BLACK

# The instructor

- **Make** notes **about what you did when you used part of a computer program.**
- **Check that your notes are in the correct order.**
- **Use your notes to help you to write** instructions **.**

> You could number each note to help.

## Instructions

Name of program _____

Name of the part used _____

Purpose _____

1 _____

2 _____

3 _____

4 _____

5 _____

6 _____

**NOW TRY THIS!**

- **Give your instructions to a friend to** test **and** edit **.**

---

**Teachers' note** Use this with any suitable software with which the children are familiar. They should focus on an activity within the program and make notes about how they used it. They can then fill out their notes as instructions to tell someone what to do, rather than as a recount of what they did.

**100% New Developing Literacy Creating and Shaping Texts: Ages 9–10**
© A & C BLACK

# Interviews to recount: 1

**A reporter interviews people about a house fire that has just been put out.**

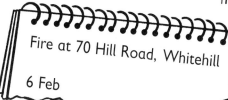

Fire at 70 Hill Road, Whitehill

6 Feb

Good evening, Mrs Roe. I'm glad to see that you and baby Max are safe. When did you first notice the fire?

About 8 o'clock. I was in the kitchen and smelled smoke so I went in the hall. Smoke was coming under the lounge door. I ran up and grabbed the baby and ran outside.

When did you call the fire brigade?

Just after eight. I heard screaming and looked out and there was Emma running with the baby.

How do you think the fire started?

A lamp in the lounge was too near the curtains. That must have started it because that part of the room was the worst burned. The bulb got very hot and the curtains caught fire.

Was anyone hurt?

No. The neighbours were right to call an ambulance because they thought someone might still be in there. Mrs Roe's quick thinking saved the baby. If she'd opened the lounge door first, the fire would have got worse. She might not have been able to get upstairs to the baby. She could have been burnt.

Is the house safe?

We've checked and there's no serious damage, just one room burned and a lot of smoke damage. It's very wet from the fire hoses, too. It's not fit to sleep in tonight.

Where will you sleep tonight?

At my mum's round the corner. She said I can stay until the house is fixed.

**Teachers' note** Use this with page 46. Ask the children to read the interview notes to find out what happened and what people said about it. They can then use the newspaper writing format on page 46 to help them to write a recount about it.

**100% New Developing Literacy
Creating and Shaping Texts:
Ages 9–10**
© A & C BLACK

# Interviews to recount: 2

- **Write a** | newspaper recount | **about the house fire at 70 Hill Road.**
- **Use information from the** | interviews |.
- **Include some** | quotations |.

Headline _____

by _____

Introduction _____

_____

*Set the scene for the reader.*

Narrative _____

_____

*Say whose house caught fire and who lived there.*

Quotation _____

_____

*Quote the householder.*

Quotation _____

_____

*Quote the neighbour.*

Narrative and reported speech _____

_____

_____

*Report what the firefighter said about the cause of the fire.*

Quotation _____

_____

*Quote the ambulance driver.*

Narrative _____

_____

*Report what the firefighter said.*

Quotation _____

_____

*Quote Emma Roe.*

Conclusion _____

_____

*Add a comment.*

**NOW TRY THIS!**

- **Read your recount with a friend. Does it answer the questions Who? Where? What? When? How?**
- | Edit | **the recount.**

**Teachers' note** Use this with page 45. Discuss the features of news recounts: the tense, person and type of language. The children should write notes in the past tense and include quotations (some direct speech and some reported). Remind them that the introduction should engage the readers' interest as well as set the scene. The headline should grab attention and say what the story is about.

**100% New Developing Literacy Creating and Shaping Texts: Ages 9–10**
© A & C BLACK

# News team

- **With your group, plan how you will collect information to write a** `news recount` **about something that has happened in your locality.**
- **Decide where you will find the information you need.**
- **Who will go to each** `source` **? Who will** `interview` **each person?**

| The event we are writing about | |
|---|---|
| Source 1 | Reporter |
| Questions | |
| Source 2 | Reporter |
| Questions | |
| Interview 1 | Reporter |
| Questions | |
| Interview 2 | Reporter |
| Questions | |

**NOW TRY THIS!**

- **Find the answers to your questions.**
- **Make** `notes` **about them.**

**Teachers' note** Use this with groups of four. Each child needs a copy of the page and the group needs a master copy, possibly on screen. They choose an event to investigate and agree a task for each reporter: two to research written/Internet sources and two to interview people. They should write notes on their section of their individual sheet. These can then be copied onto the master sheet.

100% New Developing Literacy
Creating and Shaping Texts:
Ages 9–10
© A & C BLACK

# Ghostly persuasion

**The spook police have banned the ghosts from haunting places.**

- **Use the** ⎡quotations⎤ **to help you to write an** ⎡argument⎤ **for the ghosts or the spook police.**

> Ghosts have always haunted places. It is their right.

> Ghosts have been able to haunt places for thousands of years but that doesn't mean they should do so for ever.

> What if a ghost is just walking from one place to another? We could be accused of haunting when all we are doing is going for a walk!

> Walking is fine but hanging around or loitering in places will be regarded as haunting.

> Some people enjoy meeting ghosts. We provide a valuable service.

> Many people are scared of ghosts. Scaring people counts as bullying.

> We need to educate people so that they understand that ghosts won't harm them. Then they won't be scared.

## Introduction

_____

_____

> State your opinion.

## Arguments

_____

_____

> Give reasons. Support your opinion. Say why it is right.

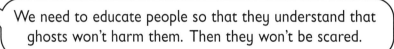

_____

_____

_____

_____

_____

## Conclusion

So _____

> Repeat your opinion.

**Teachers' note** Copy this page onto A3 paper so that the children have plenty of space to write their argument. Remind them of useful persuasive words, phrases and clauses and how to use rhetorical questions (see *Notes on the activities*, pages 11–12).

**100% New Developing Literacy
Creating and Shaping Texts:
Ages 9–10**
© A & C BLACK

# Professor Phake's lecture

Professor Phake is persuading her audience that there are people living on Mars.

- **Put the points she makes into a logical order to write her lecture.**
- Link them with persuasive words and phrases.

## Professor Phake's persuasion

| | |
|---|---|
| Scientists used to say there could be no life on Mars because there was no water. Now they admit that there is some water. | These perfect domes could not have been created naturally, |
| The photographs have never been shown in the news in case they scared people. | When people laugh at the idea of life on Mars, just remember the proof you have seen. |
| The fact that there are roads shows that there are intelligent beings. | The fact that no one has seen Martians does not mean that they do not exist. |
| A lot of information about Mars has been kept secret. I am going to tell you those secrets. | There really is life on Mars. I am about to give you some proof. |
| Look at these lines along the ground. If we zoom in we can see that they are roads – on Mars! | We have photographs from the last Mars exploration that show domed buildings. |

## Persuasive expressions

clearly

every rational person

just think for a moment

it stands to reason

it would be madness

naturally

no one could doubt

surely

the most compelling evidence

there is no doubt

why should

without a doubt

you might wonder … but

## Professor Phake's lecture

_____

_____

_____

_____

_____

_____

_____

_____

_____

**Teachers' note** Here the children pretend to be Professor Phake trying to convince people that there is life on Mars. They should think of an introduction stating what the lecture is about and indicating her point of view, then support this with arguments and sum up in a way that reinforces the opening statement. It may help some children if they cut out and order the sentences before writing.

100% New Developing Literacy
Creating and Shaping Texts:
Ages 9–10
© A & C BLACK

# The persuader

Target job _____

- **Persuade a company to let you work for them for a day.**
- **Make** `notes` **on the chart.**
- **Cut out the notes and put them in the best order.**
- **Use them to help you to write a letter.**

Think about your useful knowledge, skills and personal qualities.

| | | |
|---|---|---|
| | | |
| | | |
| | | |

Dear Sir or Madam

I would like to come and work for your company for a day as a _____

I am certain that _____

_____

_____

_____

In addition to this _____

_____

_____

_____

_____

You might think I am rather young for this work but _____

_____

_____

_____

_____

Yours faithfully _____

**Teachers' note** Ask the children to note down all the assets they think make them ideal for a particular job; also any points to counter any negative responses (for example 'too young', 'would hinder others', 'health and safety risk'). Each point should be in a separate box. They can then number the points or cut them out and put them in a logical order before writing.

**100% New Developing Literacy Creating and Shaping Texts: Ages 9–10** © A & C BLACK

# Pigeons: 1

- **Read the** facts **about pigeons.**
- **Decide what a town council should do about the thousands of pigeons that roost on buildings in the town centre.**

Discuss this with your group.

## The facts

Large numbers of pigeons in towns spread diseases, including lung disease.

Pigeon droppings and nests encourage insects such as beetles and moths.

Some people enjoy feeding and taming wild pigeons.

Some people in towns enjoy watching pigeons.

Some home-owners and business people do not like pigeon mess on their buildings.

If there is no food for pigeons they go somewhere else.

Pigeons can be scared by models of large birds (such as owls) and by electronic sounds.

Handlers of birds of prey, such as falcons, can be hired to let loose their birds to catch pigeons.

Pigeons in towns feed mainly on food waste from uncovered bins, as well as on the food people give them.

Sharp spikes or coils of wire fixed along gutters and ledges and around chimney pots stop birds landing and roosting there.

A sticky gel spread on surfaces stops pigeons landing there. They do not like the sticky feel.

It can cost about £2,000 per year to clean up pigeon mess in a town centre.

There are special cleaning materials to clean pigeon mess off stone and metal.

Animal-lovers do not like to see any birds harmed.

People cannot sit on benches in the town centre because of the pigeon mess on them.

Pigeon droppings leave pavements very slippery.

---

**NOW TRY THIS!**

- **List the** main points **you would make in a talk about pigeons in the town.**
- **Make** notes **about how you could present it to an audience.**

---

**Teachers' note** Tell the children that they are going to plan a talk on what should be done about large numbers of pigeons in a town centre. They should choose the facts that will support their argument. Different children or groups could present different solutions in order to open a class debate, ending with a vote. Use this with page 52, which provides a structure to help the children to plan their talk.

**100% New Developing Literacy Creating and Shaping Texts: Ages 9–10**
© A & C BLACK

# Pigeons: 2

- **Write a** `talk` **to say what should be done about pigeons in the town centre.**

The town centre is full of pigeons. _____

_____

_____

_____

> Say whether you welcome pigeons in the town centre.

> Explain why.

All sensible people will agree that _____

_____

_____

_____

> Say what should be done.

If these actions are taken _____

_____

_____

_____

> Say what the effects would be, and why.

There may be some who _____

_____

_____

_____

> Mention other opinion and say why they are wrong.

The main issue is _____

_____

Surely _____

_____

**NOW TRY THIS!**

- **Reread your talk.**
- **Add** `bullet points` **to help you to make your points when you present it to an audience.**

**Teachers' note** The children should first have completed page 51. Point out what the introduction is for (to state the purpose of the talk) and remind them to present the facts supporting their opinion in a way that persuades others to agree, through using persuasive language. Encourage them to mark the text to help when they read the talk: for example, with bullet points, or underlining words to stress.

**100% New Developing Literacy
Creating and Shaping Texts:
Ages 9–10
© A & C BLACK**

# Build a poem

- **Work with a group.**
- **Build a house, village or town from construction materials.**
- **Imagine the place is real.**
- **What is it like there?**
- **Make** notes **to describe it.**
- **List useful** rhyming words .
- **Write a verse modelled on 'Block City'.**

What are you able to build with your blocks?
Castles and palaces, temples and docks.
Rain may keep raining, and others go roam,
But I can be happy and building at home.

From 'Block City' by Robert Louis Stevenson

### Notes

_____

_____

_____

_____

_____

_____

_____

### Useful rhyming words

| bricks | clicks, sticks, tricks |
|---|---|
| flower(s) | hour(s), our(s), power(s), shower(s) |
| lane | again, crane, drain, main, plain, rain, train |
| | |
| | |
| | |
| | |
| | |
| | |
| | |

## Our verse

Title _____

_____ (10 syllables)

_____ (10 syllables)

_____ (10 syllables)

_____ (10–11 syllables)

---

**NOW TRY THIS!**

- **Read your verse aloud.**
- **Check the** rhythm .

Does it make sense?

What are the mood and atmosphere like?

Does the rhyme pattern work?

---

**Teachers' note** Provide construction materials such as recycled materials or kits such as Lego and ask the children to make a model town or city. They could work in groups and discuss the structures they make and what the town or village is like, its surroundings, views, industry, other work and people. Then they can make notes to help them to write a verse modelled on the example from 'Block City'.

*100% New Developing Literacy*
**Creating and Shaping Texts:**
**Ages 9–10**
© A & C BLACK

# Personify it

- **Match the examples of** | personification | **to the images.**
- **Describe the** | effect | **each personification creates.**

**a** ... shrugged off the carpet of snow and stretched their arms towards the pale sun ...

**c** ... darted its sharp glances into dusty corners ...

**b** ... silently slid around the village and slept ...

... gripped the road with its fingertips and dragged itself up the hill ...

... patiently pushing, silently nudging soil and stones aside, searching for the surface ...

**d**

**e**

| Image | Example a, b, c, d or e | Effect |
|---|---|---|
| | | |
| | | |
| | | |
| | | |
| | | |

**NOW TRY THIS!**

- **Write your own idea for personification for this image.**

**Teachers' note** The children should first have read poems in which personification is used to create effects (see *Notes on the activities*, page 12) and have had opportunities to talk about the ways in which personification can create an impression, atmosphere or feeling or a picture.

**100% New Developing Literacy Creating and Shaping Texts: Ages 9–10**
© A & C BLACK

# Early morning

- **Where do you think Grace Nichols' country village might be?**

  _____

- **How can you tell?**

  _____
  _____
  _____

- **Underline the** ⬚free verse⬚ **in the poem.**
- **Make** ⬚notes⬚ **about what you see and hear early in the morning in your locality.**
- **Write some ideas for personification.**
- **List some** ⬚expressive words⬚.

### Early Country Village Morning

Cocks crowing
Hens knowing
later they will cluck
their laying song

Houses stirring
a donkey clip-clopping
the first market bus
comes juggling along

Soon the sun will give a big yawn
and open her eye
pushing the last bit of darkness
out of the sky

_Grace Nichols_

| Notes | Personification and expressive words |
| --- | --- |
|  |  |
|  |  |
|  |  |
|  |  |
|  |  |
|  |  |

**NOW TRY THIS!**

- **Write your own 'Early Morning' poem.**
- **Give it a** ⬚title⬚ **that describes the place.**

**Teachers' note** The children should first have read poems in which personification is used to create effects (see _Notes on the activities_, page 12) and have discussed the ways in which it can intensify a feeling or atmosphere. To help them to come up with ideas, ask them to think about the effect they want (for example, speed, excitement, violence) and then imagine someone acting in these ways.

_100% New Developing Literacy_
_Creating and Shaping Texts:_
_Ages 9–10_
© A & C BLACK

# Free verse

- What | metaphor | does the poet use for her pen?

_____

- Describe how it makes you | feel |.

_____

_____

- Write your own version of the poem. Make it happy, so the pen takes off and scribbles freely.
- Write in | free verse |.

_Tonight I took the leash off my pen._

_____

_____

_____

_____

_____

_____

_____

_____

_____

_____

**Taking my Pen for a Walk**

Tonight I took the leash off my pen.
At first it was frightened,
looked up at me with confused eyes, tongue panting.
Then I said, 'Go on, run away,'
and pushed its head.
Still it wasn't sure what I wanted;
it whimpered with its tail between its legs
So I yelled, 'You're free, why don't you run –
you stupid pen, you should be glad,
now get out of my sight.'
It took a few steps.
I stamped my foot and threw a stone.
Suddenly, it realised what I was saying
and began to run furiously away from me.

_Julie O'Callaghan_

You could say what the pen writes or draws.

You could describe any sounds the pen makes. (Keep to the metaphor.)

**NOW TRY THIS!**

- **Give your poem to a friend to read aloud.**
- **Listen carefully, then mark any parts you can improve.**

**Teachers' note** Read the poem with the children. Discuss its form and rhythm and ask them about any rhyme or other effects of sounds. Draw out that the poem does not follow any formal pattern, as it is in free verse. Ask how they would change it, still using the dog metaphor and in free verse, but making the pen seem happy to be given its freedom and with the poet expressing encouragement.

**100% New Developing Literacy
Creating and Shaping Texts:
Ages 9–10**
**© A & C BLACK**

# Poetic characters

* **Act the scene with your group.**
* **Describe how the characters** feel **at different points.**

**The Traveller**

Lines 1–6

_____

_____

Lines 7–12

_____

_____

Lines 21–28

_____

_____

**The Listeners**

Lines 1–6

_____

_____

Lines 13–20

_____

_____

Lines 21–28

_____

_____

### The Listeners

'Is there anybody there?' said the Traveller,
   Knocking on the moonlit door;
And his horse in the silence champed the grasses
   Of the forest's ferny floor:
And a bird flew up out of the turret,      5
   Above the Traveller's head:
And he smote upon the door a second time;
   'Is there anybody there?' he said.
But no one descended to the Traveller;
   No head from the leaf-fringed sill      10
Leaned over and looked into his grey eyes,
   Where he stood perplexed and still.
But only a host of phantom listeners
   That dwelt in the lone house then
Stood listening in the quiet of the moonlight      15
   To that voice from the world of men:
Stood thronging the faint moonbeams on the dark stair,
   That goes down to the empty hall,
Hearkening in an air stirred and shaken
   By the lonely Traveller's call.      20
And he felt in his heart their strangeness,
   Their stillness answering his cry,
While his horse moved, cropping the dark turf,
   'Neath the starred and leafy sky;
For he suddenly smote on the door, even      25
   Louder, and lifted his head: –
'Tell them I came, and no one answered,
   That I kept my word,' he said.
Never the least stir made the listeners,
   Though every word he spake      30
Fell echoing through the shadowiness of the still house
   From the one man left awake:
Ay, they heard his foot upon the stirrup,
   And the sound of iron on stone,
And how the silence surged softly backward,      35
   When the plunging hoofs were gone.

*Walter de la Mare*

---

**NOW TRY THIS!**

* **Question 'the Traveller' and then 'the Listeners' in the hot seat.**
* **Use the questions and answers to help you to understand why they acted as they did.**

**Teachers' note** Copy this onto A3 paper. Read the poem with the children. Ask them about the atmosphere of the poem and how they think the traveller feels at the beginning. Which words express this? How do his feelings change?

100% New Developing Literacy
Creating and Shaping Texts:
Ages 9–10
© A & C BLACK

# The Traveller's thoughts

• **Write the Traveller's thoughts.**
**The first thought bubble has been filled in for you.**

It's all in darkness. Where are they? They know I'm coming.

**NOW TRY THIS!**

• **Write a** `log` **of one of the Listeners' thoughts.**

---

**Teachers' note** The children should first have completed page 57. Ask them to match the scenes to sections of the poem and to write, in the first person and present tense, what the traveller is thinking in each scene.

**100% New Developing Literacy
Creating and Shaping Texts:
Ages 9–10**
© A & C BLACK

# Another traveller

- **Plan your own poem based on 'The Listeners'.**
- **Change the** ⎡setting⎤ **to the present day.**
- **Make** ⎡notes⎤ **about the two poems.**
- **You could also use sketches and photographs.**

> The poem should be a scene from a story. It should have a feel of mystery.

| Walter de la Mare's poem | My poem |
|---|---|
| **Setting**<br>A large house, with turrets, in a forest.<br>Could have door knocker but traveller seemed to bang on it with fist 'smote'.<br>Perhaps a creeper like ivy growing on it 'leaf-fringed sill'.<br>Ferns and grass on ground. Stone path to house.<br>Night – but not dark – 'moonlight', 'moonlit door'.<br>Very quiet and still 'in the silence', 'quiet of the moonlight'. | **Setting**<br>_____<br>_____<br>_____<br>_____<br>_____<br>_____ |
| **The Traveller**<br>Age/appearance<br><br><br>How he travelled<br>Horse 'his horse in silence champed the grasses'.<br>Got off horse and left it grazing nearby while knocked on door. | **The Traveller**<br>_____<br>_____<br>_____<br>_____<br>_____<br>_____<br>_____ |
| **The Listeners** | **The Listeners**<br>_____<br>_____<br>_____<br>_____<br>_____<br>_____<br>_____<br>_____ |

**NOW TRY THIS!**

- **Write some ideas for words and phrases to use in your poem.**

**Teachers' note** The children should first have completed pages 57–58. Ask them to imagine a present-day person coming to fulfil an arranged meeting with a group of people. They could make it sinister – a derelict building or industrial estate. They could collect images online or scanned from newspapers or other sources to create a setting for their poem. A picture of 'the traveller' could be added.

**100% New Developing Literacy**
**Creating and Shaping Texts:**
**Ages 9–10**
© A & C BLACK

# Model poem

- **Write your own poem based on 'The Listeners'.**
- **Use your** boxed{notes}.
- **Try to create an** boxed{atmosphere} **of stillness and mystery.**
- **Use the** boxed{structure} **of the poem.**
- **Use some of the words from the poem.**

> Use sounds to create these effects: for example, alliteration of 's' sounds: 'smote…a second time', 'shadowiness of the still house'

Title _____

'Is there anybody there?' said _____

_____

And his/her _____

_____

And he/she _____

'Is there anybody there?' he/she said.

But no one _____

No _____

_____

_____

_____

_____

_____

_____

'Tell them _____

_____

_____

_____

> Who? Did he or she knock, call, ring a bell, use an intercom or mobile phone?

> What transport did he or she use? Where and how was it left?

> What was the place like – outside and inside? What sounds would the traveller listen out for?

> What did the traveller say?

> How did he or she leave? What sounds did this make?

---

**NOW TRY THIS!**

- **Read your poem aloud with a friend.**
- **Mark any words or phrases you can improve.**

> Think about the effects of the sounds of the words.

---

**Teachers' note** The children should first have completed pages '57–59'. It might help if they mark the parts of the poem (page 57) that need to be changed in order to model their own poems on it. The children could also key in words to use in their poems and place these on the visual images they created (page 59). They should delete whichever of 'he/she' and 'his/her' does not apply.

**100% New Developing Literacy Creating and Shaping Texts: Ages 9–10 © A & C BLACK**

# Adventures of Isabel: 1

## Adventures of Isabel

Isabel met an enormous bear,
Isabel, Isabel, didn't care;
The bear was hungry, the bear was ravenous,
The bear's big mouth was cruel and cavernous.
The bear said, Isabel, glad to meet you,
How do, Isabel, now I'll eat you!
Isabel, Isabel, didn't worry,
Isabel didn't scream or scurry.
She washed her hands and she straightened her hair up,
Then Isabel quietly ate the bear up.

Once in a night as black as pitch
Isabel met a wicked old witch.
The witch's face was cross and wrinkled,
The witch's gums with teeth were sprinkled.
Ho ho, Isabel! the old witch crowed,
I'll turn you into an ugly toad!
Isabel, Isabel, didn't worry,
Isabel didn't scream or scurry.
She showed no rage and she showed no rancour,
But she turned the witch into milk and drank her.

Isabel met a hideous giant,
Isabel continued self reliant.
The giant was hairy, the giant was horrid,
He had one eye in the middle of his forehead.
Good morning, Isabel, the giant said,
I'll grind your bones to make my bread.
Isabel, Isabel, didn't worry,
Isabel didn't scream or scurry.
She nibbled the zwieback that she always fed off,
And when it was gone, she cut the giant's head off.

Isabel met a troublesome doctor,
He punched and he poked till he really shocked her.
The doctor's talk was of coughs and chills
And the doctor's satchel bulged with pills.
The doctor said unto Isabel,
Swallow this, it will make you well.
Isabel, Isabel, didn't worry,
Isabel didn't scream or scurry.
She took those pills from the pill concocter,
And Isabel calmly cured the doctor.

*Ogden Nash*

- **Underline or circle the parts of this poem that make it good to** [ read aloud ].
- **Complete the key, using lines of different colours.**
- **Make notes about the** [ pattern ] **of each verse.**
- **Use arrows or lines to link the notes to the verses.**

### Key

repeated lines
repeated ideas
effective end of line rhyme

### Notes about the pattern of each verse

**NOW TRY THIS!**

- **Plan how to read the poem aloud in a group of four.**

You could annotate another copy of the poem.

**Teachers' note** Ask the children to read the poem with their groups and to mark it as suggested on the page to help them to read it aloud with expression. They should consider how many voices should read each part. Reading it aloud should help them to make notes about the pattern of each verse (rhyme, rhythm, repetition).

100% New Developing Literacy
Creating and Shaping Texts:
Ages 9–10
© A & C BLACK

- **On the notepad, try out ideas for completing the skeleton verse.**
- **Choose the ones you think sound best.**
- **Complete the rhyme.**

The rhyme-bank will help. Add other rhymes of your own.

**Notes**

_____

_____

_____

_____

_____

_____

_____

_____

_____

| **Rhyme-bank** | |
|---|---|
| another | mother, brother |
| better | get her, ate her, met her |
| corner | warn her, scorn her |
| cracker, lacquer, packer | smack her, whack her |
| factor, tractor | smacked her, whacked her |
| farmer | harm her |
| gorilla, killer, miller | chill her, kill her, thrill her |
| malice | palace |
| sorrow | tomorrow |
| teacher | reach her |
| troll | bowl, coal, hole, pole, whole |

Isabel met a _____ ,

Isabel _____ .

The _____ was _____ , the _____ was _____ ,

The _____ was _____ .

The _____ said, 'Isabel _____ ,

I'll _____ ,

Isabel, Isabel didn't worry,

Isabel didn't scream or scurry.

She _____ ,

And _____ .

**NOW TRY THIS!**

- **Read your verse aloud with a friend and** edit **it.**

**Teachers' note** The children should first have read and marked the poem on page 61, as suggested on the page. Ask them to use what they have learned to help them to make up their own verse, using the skeleton verse as a framework and the rhyme-bank to help them to find suitable rhymes. Encourage them to try out their ideas aloud with a friend.

**100% New Developing Literacy Creating and Shaping Texts: Ages 9–10** © A & C BLACK

# Performance poet

- **Plan your own** `performance poem` **using 'Adventures of Isabel' as a model.**
- **Make up a new character. Instead of meeting other characters he or she could go to dangerous or exciting places.**
- **Think about what the character might do or collect there.**

| **Character** | **Places visited** |
|---|---|
| Name | |
| Description | |
| | |
| Amusing or interesting characteristics | What the character does or collects there |
| _Fearless? Clumsy? Funny? Forgetful? Vain? Other?_ | _Food? Gadgets? Pets? Other things?_ |

### Poem plan

| | |
|---|---|
| Number of verses | Rhyme pattern and examples |
| Number of lines per verse | |
| Repetition and examples | |
| _Vowels? Consonants? Words? Phrases?_ | _Couplets? Alternate lines? Every fourth line? Other?_ |
| Ideas for chorus | Rhythm |

**NOW TRY THIS!**

- **Write the first verse of your poem.**
- **Read it aloud with a friend and** `edit` **it.**
- **Use this to help you to write the second verse.**

**Teachers' note** The children should first have completed pages 61–62 and will need a copy of the poem 'Adventures of Isabel'. Ask them to think up their own character and to write descriptive notes about him or her, including personal qualities: Isabel was fearless but the new character might be forgetful, vain or clumsy. Then they can imagine places this character goes and what happens there.

**100% New Developing Literacy
Creating and Shaping Texts:
Ages 9–10**
© A & C BLACK

# Performance evaluator

- **Evaluate a** performance **of a poem.**
- **How well did the performance bring out:**

| the mood of the poem: humorous, sad, exciting, mysterious? | the meaning of the poem? | changes in atmosphere? | build-up of tension, story, character, mystery? |

Poem _____ by _____

| Points to think about | How they were used | Effects |
|---|---|---|
| Volume (loud voices, quiet voices, changes in volume) | | |
| Pace (fast, slow, changes in pace) | | |
| Expression (using voices to express feelings, mood, atmosphere) | | |
| Facial expressions | | |
| Movement | | |
| Other (for example, sound effects, props, costume, masks) | | |

**NOW TRY THIS!**

- **Write one suggestion that would improve this performance.**
- **Explain how it would help.**

**Teachers' note** The children can use this page to help them to identify the criteria by which to judge the performance of a poem. They can also use these criteria to help them to plan a performance. Ask them to experiment with their voices, facial expressions and movements in order to find the most effective.

**100% New Developing Literacy
Creating and Shaping Texts:
Ages 9–10**
© A & C BLACK